<u>Positive</u>

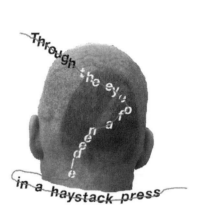

ISBN: 979-8-9871573-8-1

Positive Introduction

- tENTATIVELY, a cONVENIENCE
- October 4, 2024E.V.

It's now over 19 years since I started my **Positive diary**. Its genesis was in talks that my new friend Julie Gonzalez & I had about our mutual negative attitudes. We were both a bit disgusted with ourselves. I proposed that we write Positive diaries - the idea was that we'd keep diaries of only the things that were positive in our days in order to try to change our attitudes to appreciate these positive things instead of being complainers. I started this on August 1st, 2005 & continued it for a whole year until July 31st, 2006 - then I put the results aside & didn't think about the project much after that - it had served its purpose.

However, occasionally, in conversation I

mention it as a way to try to improve one's life. My memory of the diary was that it was somewhat boring. I finally decided to revisit it recently & to reread the whole thing to determine if I'd find it worthy of publication. I was a bit surprised by what I found. Even though I was working for a pittance & barely surviving financially & even though my love life was a complicated floundering mess, *I actually had a substantial social life*. Rereading the entries I'm astounded at how much time I spent with friends. I was 52 during most of this time, I'm 71 as I write this. At 71 I have almost *no social life at all*. This has much to do with the destructive force of the quarantine & lockdown that started in 2020 but it may have even more to do with aging & agism. Many of my women friends had children & settled into an insular family life, others of them became menopausal & lost what little lust they had for me. &, of course, when I didn't take the bait I wasn't of any further interest either.

Be that as it may, my attempted positive attitude did persevere in a mutated form. Sometime after 2006, I don't remember when, I started emailing out **Annual Reports** to my Bulk Friends Email List on January 1st of each year. The idea has been to list my accomplishments of the year just ended in order to make myself feel better about what had often been very grim & lonely times. Here's a sample one summarizing 2018, it's the earliest one I could find so maybe it was the 1st - I've removed the concluding image from it so that this book will be without images:

My 2018

Like most years of my life, 2018 was full of huge disappointments & deprivations counterbalanced by substantial accomplishments. "My 2018" is the outline of these latter, collected here to put a positive spin on the year.

I read & reviewed 77 books.

I made 74 movies, 11 of which are feature-length.

I played 49 duets (+ 8 mini-duets done for the camera); 2 trios; & 4 quartets (+ 1 mini-quartet done for the camera) involving 39 collaborators (including the ones for the mini-sessions).*

I made 50 new web-pages.

I gave 11 'performances'.

I had 10 audio pieces published (online, with the exception of 1 cassette compilation).

I gave 8 screenings (2 more are included under 'performances').

I organized the 4 day, 3 venue, UNDERAPPRECIATED MOVIEMAKERS FESTIVAL.

I had one piece published in a hard copy book.

I survived on less than the official US $12,140 poverty level.

- tENTATIVELY, a cONVENIENCE; December 31, 2018

* Here's a list of the collaborators in chronological appearance + (the number of times we played together):

Anthony Osborne (1)
Pamelia Stickney (1)
Lezet (2)
Marco Lucchi (2)
Ben Opie (5)
Noah Rectenwald (1)
Caleb Gamble (1)
Jim Storch (1)
Rich Randall (1)
Dick Turner (10)
Coal Hornet (3)
Little Fyodor (1)
Slavek Kwi (1)
Kenny Haney (8)
Alex Stanton (1)
Roger Dannenberg (3)
Hyla Willis (1)
Devin Sherman (1)
Warren Burt (1)
Michael Pestel (1)
Eric Lipsky (1)
Tom DiVenti (1)
Unfinished Symphonies (2)
Spat Cannon (1)
Skizz Cyzyk (3)
Neely Bruce (1)

William Davison (1)
San Salamandra (1)
Jason Belcher (1)
Michael Boyd (1)
AG Davis (1)
Stephen Bradley (1)
Jeff Weston (2)
dzum (4)
Florian Cramer (2)
Breen Casey (2)
Tanya Solomon (1)
Anonymous (1)
Joy Toujours (1)

****

Here's a list of links relevant to the BIG PROJECT of the year: "365", the project for which I shot footage every day of my playing (M)Usic. This was very ambitious & I'm extremely satisfied with the results so I hope that you can take the time out to witness all of "365" (see the links below) or, at least, selected parts of it.

2018 Month Movie URLs

"January, 2018": https://youtu.be/

aVJpvfu3M1w

"February, 2018": https://youtu.be/HeVPbxhA7Cc

"March, 2018": https://youtu.be/gavFY6NEUCU

"April, 2018": https://youtu.be/jKbgyKL-7hs

"May, 2018": https://youtu.be/-fNMKjIiKxc

"June, 2018": https://youtu.be/5eLDrLx9cjU

"July, 2018": https://youtu.be/BD6wcoE92L4

"August, 2018": https://youtu.be/nlvmltj_v7I

"September, 2018": https://youtu.be/uW2KiTweHD8

"October, 2018": https://youtu.be/ytUixRI8bqA

"November, 2018": https://youtu.be/

wDYxiMzNLxM

"December, 2018": https://youtu.be/77xlr8hSsXU

365:

https://youtu.be/ZaglhRjJYzU

https://archive.org/details/idioideo_verizon_365

+ duets, quartets, related performances, & at least one other related collaboration:

"2018.06.01 duet with Ben Opie - Pittsburgh, PA - in person"
- uploaded to my onesownthoughts YouTube channel on June 16, 2018, here: https://youtu.be/I8vngkQtrt8
& to the Internet Archive on the same day: https://archive.org/details/2018.06.01Ben

"2018.06.02 duet with Noah Rectenwald - Pittsburgh, PA - in person"
- uploaded to my onesownthoughts YouTube channel on June 18, 2018, here: https://youtu.be/CH67VT5McGs
& to the Internet Archive on the same day: https://archive.org/details/2018.06.02Noah

"2018.06.03 duet with Caleb Gamble - Pittsburgh, PA - in person"
- uploaded to my onesownthoughts YouTube channel on June 20, 2018, here: https://youtu.be/HyyR32b-QCU
& to the Internet Archive on the same day: https://archive.org/details/2018.06.03Caleb

"2018.06.04 duet with Jim Storch - Pittsburgh, PA - in person"
- uploaded to my onesownthoughts YouTube channel on June 22, 2018, here:
https://youtu.be/ErfvcYsVTMY
& to the Internet Archive on the same day:
https://archive.org/details/2018.06.04Jim

"2018.06.05 duet with Rich Randall - Pittsburgh, PA - in person"
- uploaded to my onesownthoughts YouTube channel on June 24, 2018, here:
https://youtu.be/bJZVdmssFDA
& to the Internet Archive on the same day:
https://archive.org/details/2018.06.05Rich

"2018.06.06 duet with Dick Turner - Paris, France - via file exchange"
- uploaded to my onesownthoughts YouTube channel on June 26, 2018, here:
https://youtu.be/_sNrKmaiYmY
& to the Internet Archive on the same day:
https://archive.org/details/2018.06.06Dick

"2018.06.07 duet with Coal Hornet - Pittsburgh, PA - in person"
- uploaded to my onesownthoughts YouTube channel on June 28, 2018, here:
https://youtu.be/0BqliMfTxhM

& to the Internet Archive on the same day:
https://archive.org/details/2018.06.07CoalHornet

"2018.06.08 duet with Little Fyodor - Denver, CO - via Skype"
- uploaded to my onesownthoughts YouTube channel on June 30, 2018, here:
https://youtu.be/droAU62tfA8
& to the Internet Archive on the same day:
https://archive.org/details/2018.06.08LittleFyodor

"2018.06.09 duet with Slavek Kwi (Artificial Memory Trace) - Ireland - 'telepathically' (involving file exchange)"
- uploaded to my onesownthoughts YouTube channel on July 2, 2018, here:
https://youtu.be/7e_jY_cb0no
& to the Internet Archive on the same day:
https://archive.org/details/2018.06.09SlavekKwi

"2018.06.10 duet with Kenny Haney - Pittsburgh, PA - in person"
- uploaded to my onesownthoughts YouTube channel on July 4, 2018, here:
https://youtu.be/qTaN1zyRzPA
& to the Internet Archive on the same day:
https://archive.org/details/2018.06.10Kenny

"2018.06.11 duet with Alex Stanton - Pittsburgh, PA - in person"
- uploaded to my onesownthoughts YouTube channel on July 6, 2018, here:
https://youtu.be/DRfKdm5YLQ0
& to the Internet Archive on the same day:
https://archive.org/details/2018.06.11Alex

"2018.06.12 duet with Roger Dannenberg - Pittsburgh, PA - in person"
- uploaded to my onesownthoughts YouTube channel on July 8, 2018, here:
https://youtu.be/uD3i755cqPg
& to the Internet Archive on the same day:
https://archive.org/details/2018.06.12Roger

"2018.06.13 duet with Hyla Willis - Pittsburgh, PA - in person"
- uploaded to my onesownthoughts YouTube channel on July 10, 2018, here:
https://youtu.be/bo9CKfjzNWU
& to the Internet Archive on the same day:
https://archive.org/details/2018.06.13Hyla

"2018.06.14 duet with Devin Sherman - Pittsburgh, PA - in person"
- uploaded to my onesownthoughts YouTube channel on July 12, 2018, here:
https://youtu.be/OBAhNYmN658

& to the Internet Archive on the same day:
https://archive.org/details/2018.06.14Devin

"2018.06.15 duet with Warren Burt - Australia - via Skype"
- uploaded to my onesownthoughts YouTube channel on July 14, 2018, here:
https://youtu.be/6DJRuxzjz8Q
& to the Internet Archive on the same day:
https://archive.org/details/2018.06.15Warren

"2018.06.16 duet with Michael Pestel - Middleton, CT - via FaceTime"
- uploaded to my onesownthoughts YouTube channel on July 16, 2018, here:
https://youtu.be/cNQDKLqeK34
& to the Internet Archive on the same day:
https://archive.org/details/2018.06.16Michael

"2018.06.17 duet with Eric Lipsky - Pittsburgh, PA - in person"
- uploaded to my onesownthoughts YouTube channel on July 18, 2018, here:
https://youtu.be/c6o8ixWg4RA
& to the Internet Archive on the same day:
https://archive.org/details/2018.06.17Eric

"2018.06.18 duet with Tom DiVenti - Eastern Pennsylvania - via FaceTime"

- uploaded to my onesownthoughts
YouTube channel on July 20, 2018, here:
https://youtu.be/4p7EfpowkLA
& to the Internet Archive on the same day:
https://archive.org/details/2018.06.18Tom

"2018.06.19 duet with Unfinished Symphonies - Pittsburgh, PA - in person"
- uploaded to my onesownthoughts
YouTube channel on July 22, 2018, here:
https://youtu.be/fljzUuSCQtc
& to the Internet Archive on the same day:
https://archive.org/details/2018.06.19Rob

"2018.06.20 duet with Spat Cannon - Leeds, England - via Skype"
- uploaded to my onesownthoughts
YouTube channel on July 24, 2018, here:
https://youtu.be/Qb0UPboWnbk
& to the Internet Archive on the same day:
https://archive.org/details/2018.06.20Spat

"2018.06.21 duet with Ben Opie - Pittsburgh, PA - in person"
- uploaded to my onesownthoughts
YouTube channel on July 26, 2018, here:
https://youtu.be/KfDnnPqIH_A
& to the Internet Archive on the same day:
https://archive.org/details/2018.06.21Ben

"2018.06.22 duet with Skizz Cyzyk - BalTimOre, MD - via Skype"
- uploaded to my onesownthoughts YouTube channel on July 28, 2018, here:
https://youtu.be/uTWI5d5GEjc
& to the Internet Archive on the same day:
https://archive.org/details/2018.06.22Skizz

"2018.06.23 duet with Neely Bruce - Middleton, CT - via Skype"
- uploaded to my onesownthoughts YouTube channel on July 30, 2018, here:
https://youtu.be/RG9hAspi9Qw
& to the Internet Archive on the same day:
https://archive.org/details/2018.06.23Neely

"2018.06.24 duet with William Davison - Toronto, Canada - via Skype (FB version)"
- uploaded to my onesownthoughts YouTube channel on August 1, 2018, here:
https://youtu.be/DR7tT77Lbu8
& to the Internet Archive on the same day:
https://archive.org/details/2018.06.24William

"2018.06.25 duet with San Salamandra - Pittsburgh, PA - in person"
- uploaded to my onesownthoughts YouTube channel on August 3, 2018, here:

https://youtu.be/09d0pD5ZZMY
& to the Internet Archive on the same day:
https://archive.org/details/
2018.06.25SanSalamandra

"2018.06.26 duet with Jason Belcher - Pittsburgh, PA - in person"
- uploaded to my onesownthoughts YouTube channel on August 5, 2018, here:
https://youtu.be/Hz2hzuvnH9k
& to the Internet Archive on the same day:
https://archive.org/details/2018.06.26Jason

"2018.06.27 duet with Michael Boyd - Pittaburgh, PA - in person"
- uploaded to my onesownthoughts YouTube channel on August 7, 2018, here:
https://youtu.be/WmChx3AoRo4
& to the Internet Archive on the same day:
https://archive.org/details/
2018.06.27MichaelBoyd

"2018.06.28 duet with AG Davis - Florida - via Skype"
- uploaded to my onesownthoughts YouTube channel on August 9, 2018, here:
https://youtu.be/RTVYv8yRBjU
& to the Internet Archive on the same day:
https://archive.org/details/2018.06.28AG

"2018.06.29 duet with Stephen Bradley - BalTimOre, MD - via FaceTime"
- uploaded to my onesownthoughts YouTube channel on August 11, 2018, here: https://youtu.be/94oRrRpviYs
& to the Internet Archive on the same day: https://archive.org/details/2018.06.29Stephen

"2018.06.30 duet with Jeff Weston - Pittsburgh, PA - in person"
- uploaded to my onesownthoughts YouTube channel on August 13, 2018, here: https://youtu.be/UF-YSbGK0nE
& to the Internet Archive on the same day: https://archive.org/details/2018.06.30Jeff

"uni.Sol_II.tENT"
- uploaded to my onesownthoughts YouTube channel in an extremely compressed form on July 15, 2018, here: https://youtu.be/Sjg-C-Ay9MA

"Boning Up"
- uploaded to the Internet Archive August 11, 2018: https://archive.org/details/BoningUp

"4 X 2"
- uploaded to my onesownthoughts

YouTube channel August 12, 2018: https://youtu.be/1v2B4LgivH0

"**3 X 4**"
- uploaded to my onesownthoughts YouTube channel September 28, 2018: https://youtu.be/FPtoafTKbBA

"**2018.12.06 tENT-Weston**"
- on my onesownthoughts YouTube channel December 10, 2018 here: https://youtu.be/j4vwPXLPLNg

"**Filibuster**"
- uploaded to my onesownthoughts YouTube channel on December 12, 2018 here: https://youtu.be/7iU87E_2Y2s

"**1 X 4**"
- uploaded to my onesownthoughts YouTube channel on December 30, 2018: https://youtu.be/nLz-bOpLRRk "

****

I sent these emails out to friends partially in the hope of initiating conversations, I hoped that people would tell me about what they'd done that year. I only got replies from 2 or 3 friends, usually very brief ones. It's possible that these emailings went straight to spam folders because they were Bcc:ed to the recipients, &, therefore, never seen as a result. It's also possible that my years have been embarrassingly more productive than those of my friends so that they were simply annoyed at what could be construed as bragging on my part.

In the recent past, in mid 2024, I've started manifesting positivity in a way that took me by surprise. I started feeling intense delight in response to a variety of everyday type things, it's as if I've developed an appreciation for life on its own. One night I pulled a blanket over me because a fall chill had set in &, suddenly, I realized what an amazing & pleasant sensation that additional warmth was. Another time, I was walking in an urban environment & I looked up & saw the sun on a building & found it extremely beautiful. I drank a glass of water & was stunned by how perfect it was. I walked around a reservoir & was in near-ecstasy at the pleasure of seeing unpolluted water. I saw two Mourning Doves cuddling with each other on my roof for a week solid & was deeply touched. I went for a walk in autumn weather & felt amazingly cleansed & refreshed by the temperate temperature & the clear air & sunny sky & the quiet. All of these things might seem too simple & commonplace to some but, to me, I realized that if one takes them for granted then one is missing key pleasures.

SO, here I am in the early fall of 2024, age 71. My life of the last years or even decades seem so deprived of love & financial adequacy that it's easy to be negative. Nonetheless, looking back on 2005 & 2006 & realizing that I felt much the same way at the time but that, in retrospect, my life then seems almost fantastically positive & I wonder what this year would look like to my future self reading it at age 90 (which I have little reason to believe I'll make it to). It's quite possible that if I kept a Positive diary for age 71 (which I admit to having no intention of doing) I might find my life to be absolutely incredible in retrospect!

SOO, welcome to my **Positive diary**: what I hope you'll get out it is a sense of how such a simple activity can have a potentially profound effect on one's feelings about one's life. Ha ha! I detest 'Self-Help' books but this comes as close as I'll ever get to writing one. Chances are, you won't know many or any of the people mentioned but that doesn't necessarily matter - reading this may stimulate you to think of your own friends, your own activities, & to realize that no matter how bad your overall life may seem at times there's probably a silver lining. Of course, even at my worst, my life has actually been pretty good in contrast to the lives of people in prison, of people living on the streets, of people with drug addiction problems, with severe physical afflictions, etc - so, really, what am I complaining about?! I have enough trouble putting a positive spin on my own life with my own problems with severe alienation from other people & with living under the poverty line - what would I do if I had the problems that I see other people having in the world around me?! My positive-spin abilities would be severely challenged &, probably, defeated. I don't want to find out, I'm close to my limit as it is.

Positive

Monday, August 1st, 2005EV

I'm starting this diary.
I don't have to work today, SO
I can sleep as late as I can manage & whenever &
I can prepare the "Story of a Fructiferous Society" packages to be mailed off &
I can mail the packages off &
I can go to do the photocopying I haven't had time for recently &
I can catch up on my e-mailing &
I can contact the new real estate agent.
ALSO, I have what is for me an unusual abundance of money.
My CD burner is still working so I'm getting closer to finishing the "RATical RATio - pRAT 2" project.
Julie's expressed interest in keeping a similar diary so I may have company w/ this.
I'm enjoying this.
I have a slew of new movies & bks to check out &
Greg gave me a set of Math filmstrips yesterday to check out & possibly use for PNT purposes.
I have plenty of blank DVDs & DVD cases & printer ink so I can keep making "Story.." DVDs.
I ate at Lulus (delish!) & have leftovers.
I saw John Doran (very nice guy).

I finally got started on the Cuban Anarchists project.
Helped an old woman use a photocopier.
I got some Pineapple/Coconut drink (delish!).
I thought of so many things to be positive about while I was out that there're too many to write down.
Was thinking about how glad I am that the anarchist 'institutions':
      Food Not Bombs, Free Ride, Book 'Em, the Big Idea - are thriving in P-Burgh.
Helped Mike figure out whether he was getting a good price for his silver pro trumpet.
Kim e-mailed proposing we do something together this wk.
Cathy Cook from UMBC e-mailed back about "Story..".
Julie called me back & we talked about our POSITIVE diaries.
Took a bath.
Listened to Czech & Bulgarian music - inspired by Germaine's e-mail.
Had a good talk w/ Ben Shannon about the abusiveness of Cirque de Soleil management & other things.
Burned 10 "Story.." DVDs & a slew of "RATical..2" CDs.
Checked out "Best of A/V Geeks IV" DVD.
Read some Bruno Schulz.
Thought of new recordings publication series: RexLax
Didn't drink alcohol.

Tuesday, August 2nd, 2005EV

No new bug bites.
No sign of the rat(?) since I plugged the probable entry hole w/ concrete & broken glass.
Ate something different from my usual fare: grapes, orange, sweet potato pancake, etc..
Sent off 2 more packages.
Encountered Austin Skot! on way to Frick & made arrangements to interview him @ Book 'Em on Sunday.
Encountered Michael Pestel's friend Linda on way to Frick & she gave me directions.
Got hired by the Frick & put in a plug for Julie to get work there too.
Made plans w/ Julie to go on bike ride on the "jail trail" - wch I've never ridden on.
Julie & I explored - including Greenfield - a neighborhood I'd consider living in.

Wednesday, August 3rd, 2005EV

Went to help Barb Antel build a shed
    - thinking I might just do it as a favor or just charge her a nominal fee.
    - She then pd me $140! w/o my asking for that much & then wdn't accept my lower offer(s).

Thursday, August 4th, 2005EV

Sent off more packages.
Used the unexpected money from the day before to justify 'treating' myself to 3 CDs & eating out.
After having had air-conditioners for at least 25 yrs w/o ever using one I installed one
      & have felt great relief from the stupor I've been in in this heat.
Kim came by & we watched Ken Russell's <u>The Devils</u> wch I hadn't seen for a long time & wch was GREAT.
Still cranking out the CDs.

Friday, August 5th, 2005EV

Updated some web-sites slightly.
Updating this POSITIVE slightly (I hadn't written in it the past 2 days).
The film I'm screening tonight is in good shape so there probably won't be any problems.
Used more of the money from Barb to get 8 more movies & to eat out again.
Have developed a new interest over the past few days: Senoi Dream Theory & Kilton Stewart
      & the related controversy. Am in the process of reading G. William Domhoff's critcism of Stewart
      & read Stewart's article in <u>Altered States of Consciousness</u>.
Screened <u>Mandingo</u> at the Warhol. It's an intense look at slavery & its related oppressions & suppressions.
THEN returned home & cheked out Miike's <u>Dead or Alive</u>.

Saturday, August 6th, 2005EV

etta surprised me w/ a phone call "just to chat" from Virginia.
Finished making 10 more "Story.." DVDs.
Kim & pianist friend Andrew accompanied me on a bike exploration of Perrysville Ave culminating in
    looking at a large house for sale.
We further explored St James Landing where we crossed paths w/ David Pohl.
Edited the 1st RexLax CD: "RATical RATio - pRAT 3".

Sunday, August 7th, 2005EV

I started writing my essay on "30 4 5 + 97.9" - inspired by one version of the sound piece being on the CD
    that I finished editing yesterday.
I listened to the "RATical RATio - pRAT 3" CD & liked it (surprise, surprise, eh?).
I shot etta interviewing Scot! from Austin re the bks-to-prisoners program he's associated w/
    - as a part of my Book 'Em documentary.
Pippi Longstocking (Robert) & Dweezle (Laura) visited post their annual pilgramage to
    the Twins Convention. I hadn't seen them in something like 20 yrs.
    It was a great pleasure & I got to screen

"Story of a Fructiferous Society" for them
& to give them each copies of it.

Monday, August 8th, 2005EV

I made substantial progress on the "30 4 5 + 97.9" essay.
I made a Czech Music tape for Germ.
I dumped the Scot! interview into my computer.
Kim & Andrew joined me for dinner.
As usual, I have the luxury of drinking wine & watching a movie as my late-nite relaxation.

Tuesday, August 9th, 2005EV

Andrew, the real estate agent, called me today & set up an appointment for tomorrow.
Continued work on the "30 4 5 + 97.9" essay.
Lewis Jackson phoned me & told me he watched "Story of a Fructiferous Scoiety" last Saturday
    & that he loved it! & that he thought it was very elegant
    - & he asked for me to send him 3 more copies so that
    he cd send them to the Modern & PS1 & someplace on the west coast where he thought they'd be
    interested in it. THANK YOU LEWIS!
Visited Margaret in the hospital - she seems to

be recuperating well.
Finished burning the last of the 500 "RATical RATio - pRAT 2" CDs - after 8 mnths!
Didn't drink any alcohol.
Edited both volumes of the Ivo Malec restrospective for Germ.

Wednesday, August 10th, 2005EV

Continued making "pond(er)" CDs.
Sent off the package for Germ & the package for Lewis.
Enjoyed the luxury of eating out.
Got materials for making "pond(er)" CD packages & printed them out.
Got Kyle Gann CD from library.
George Davis returned my calls & sd he'd push for screening "Story.." for 2 nites at the Nov 2005
        Three Rivers Film Festival. THANK YOU GEORGE!
Visited Margaret in the hospital & took her a burritto & 8 movies.
Ran into Max (traveller from Pig Town) who I hadn't seen for a yr or so.
Finished watching the last of the 10 volume VHS horror movie set.
Didn't drink alcohol.

[3:30AM: I've noted a few things in the process of writing this POSITIVE:
I've deliberately exaggerated my negativity in order to 'justify' this - but I've already got these

'positive' habits built into my usual attitude. ALSO, as Julie & I've already (sortof) discussed somewhat, the criteria for what's 'positive' is ambiguous: what gets included? what gets excluded? Semi-banal aspects of the day can be either: I can, eg, list what movie(s) I watch or not OR list what music I listen to or not OR list what I read or not OR list what I eat or not. At least I'm not in prison, at least I'm not being spectacularly brutalized. My (social) environment is mostly friendly. All in all, even though some very important levels of affection are missing from my life, I am very, VERY lucky. I can't afford health care but (even though my teeth are decaying slightly & I worry that I may have hepatitus C & the beginnings of glaucoma) my health is generally better than most people's my age & of many people much younger. I don't even wear glasses!]

I've been unable to sleep but I've been thinking & inspired.

A little while ago, I realized very clearly that thoughts I was having existed in a completely functional PRE-LINGUISTIC state. In other words, I was having a thought that was completely understandable to myself THAT WAS NOT FORMED INTO WORDS OR ORGANIZED GRAMMATICALLY. I then decided to put it into words & sentences but as I was doing so I realized that that was UNNECESSARY for that thought to be fully understandable in my mind. Forming it into a sentence was simply another way of having the thought exist but not the thought itself. Strangely, I don't recall ever

having had this revelation before even though
my mind must be continually in the midst of this
pre/sub-lingual process. This strikes me as
potentially very important & a sort of personal
resolution (or quasi-resolution) of what I suspect
is a primary philosophical debate: is language
'necessary' for thought? NO. Is thought, by
definition, organized as language? NO. I think I
wd've always answered NO to these questions
INSTINCTUALLY but the feeling of having
consciously experienced this pre/sub-lingual
thought is now concrete to me.

I'm still trying to think of a name for the 'club'
that I proposed to Kalie Tuesday:
a club for turning memory & vocabulary
improvement into a social activity:
I've thought of VOCABUMEMORY or MEMOLARY
as obvious contractions OR (just now):
OBVIOUS CONTRACTIONS but none of these
names are quite satisfactory.
The 'club' won't exist until it has a name. It can
address my obvious disatisfaction w/
vocabulary stimulation in my conversational life &
my 'theory' that socializing helps keep
cross-referencing neural pathways open & busy -
hence better memory.
The basic idea is to have periodic social
gatherings at wch the main requirements are
that every participant tell a story involving a
particular word that most people present
aren't likely to know. The narrative is meant to
help imprint the word. Hence a memory
experiment.
By the end of the gathering it's hoped that
everyone will have learned all the new words.

These new words shd probably also be expected to be accumulatively used in successive gatherings.

ALSO, given that I 'want' to get some dental work done & that I've previously had the inspiration to get it done in Canada as a 'performance' / to make a movie, I realized that a Department of Dentistry might be a good thing to present as part of the November Toronto Dept Fest. I envision a group of core participants encircling a dentist filling my right front incisor & replacing my cap - watching it as a performance &, of course, 'excessively' quasi-documenting it. I must remember to write AMEN! proposing this so that an appropriate dentist can be found.

Just ordered bks by Giordano Bruno & Raymond Llull [alternate spelling] on-line.
Listening to Kyle Gann's music (possibly for the 1st time).

Thursday, August 11th, 2005EV

Grocery shopped (something I'd procrastinated on).
Did all the scanning from Erok's materials for the Radical History Bike Tour quasi-documentary.
Finshed making 20 "pond(er)" CDs.

Friday, August 12th, 2005EV

Got 2 e-mails from 'Rina Steinhauer today (short-term lover from 21 yrs ago)!
Mainly worked on "30 4 5 + 97.9" essay wch I can probably finish w/in a wk.
There was either a bird or a bat in the house tonite wch, fortunately, flew out thru the open door.
Now it's time to watch <u>Timothy Leary's Dead</u> & drink some wine before going to sleep.

Saturday, August 13th, 2005EV

Finished reading Bruno Schulz's <u>Sanitorium under the Sign of the Hourglass</u>.
Went to Home Movie Nite at Greg & Alisa's.
Made plans w/ Rachel (Angry Ron's ex) to go bike riding Wednesday @ 10AM.
Back home, I hung out w/ Alexi, etta, Andalusia, Mary Mac, & Erok.

Sunday, August 14th, 2005EV

Finished my "30 4 5 + 97.9" essay.
Didn't drink any alcohol.

Monday, August 15th,

2005EV

Organized a list of houses to look at.
Finished reading The Films of Paul Morrisey.
Had Rachel Weber & truck'o'kids give me passing very friendly greeting.
Rode around w/ Andrew the Impaler figuring out housing possibilities.
Watched Hong Kong(?) 'Black Comedy' Ebola Syndrome & got drunk on sake.

Tuesday, August 16th, 2005EV

Rc'vd the Doctor Illuminatus - A Raymond Llull Reader bk in the mail.
Rode thru the Hill District no my bike for the 1st time since I've lived in Pittsburgh(!) to explore
    - after looking at the outside of 101 Roberts St.
Went to the library.
Talked w/ Scot (of Scot & Aaron) outside for awhile.
Got a few things from the Indian store.
Rode bikes back to Polish Hill w/ Aloytious [sp?] - friendly neighbor.
Organized & e-mailed a list of the properties I'm interested in to Andrew.
E-mailed Kyle Gann about Low Classical Usic.
Wrote a long e-mail to Germ & brainstormed about a new e-mail identity.
Watched the 1st 3 selections of the A/V Geeks

comp: "Anatomy of a Brat".
Recorded a few more audio parts of my "30 4 5 + 97.9" lecture.
Didn't drink any alcohol.

Wednesday, August 17th, 2005EV

Rachel didn't come for our proposed bike ride.

[As noted last Wednesday, what's positive or negative can be ambiguous. The situation w/ Rachel is a perfect example. On Saturday, when she asked me to go on a bike trip w/ her it was positive that someone wanted to do something w/ me. Today, when she didn't arrive at the agreed-upon time I was somewhat relieved because I hadn't felt like getting up so early to rush out & ride a bike - so her non-arrival was also positive. More & more I realize that this really has become my typical attitude because, w/ the accumulated experience of the unreliability of other people, I've come to not expect much from others so it's built into my attitude that if others don't meet my expectations then it's positive for me not to be relying on them & I detach myself.]

Finished making the 30 4 5 + 97.9 lecture examples CD.
Rc'vd Giordano Bruno's The Expulsion of the Triumphant Beast bk in the mail.
Finished burning 5 more "Hitting Things - Volume 1" CDs & started working on burning Volume 2.

Made VD-RADIO tape order for Pippi.
Worked on transferring TESTES-3 Library B end from reel-to-reel to CD.
Watched the last of the A/V Geeks' <u>Anatomy of Brat</u> comp.
Watched <u>FLY Jefferson Airplane</u>.

Thursday, August 18th, 2005EV

Finished tidying the TESTES-3 Library B end transfer & made a packaged CD - started on Library C/E.
Went house hunting w/ Andrew the Impaled & learned that he's in the Church of the SubGenius!
Watched the last of the A/V Geeks DVDs: <u>Blackboard Bungle</u>.

Friday, August 19th, 2005EV

Julie called from Baltimore.
Continued working on TESTES-3 transfers.
Worked (slightly) on the very hypothetical gig w/ Michael Evans & Daniel Higgs.
Finally got to see the Jack Smith / Andy Warhol <u>Batman/Dracula</u>.

Saturday, August 20th, 2005EV

Went to Duke's & Kalie & Kelly & Mark & his bro

& dad were there.
      [Can you tell I'm writing this on Tuesday & that I've already forgotten what I did this day?]

Sunday, August 21st, 2005EV

Finally studied the DEVO DVD that I got from the library.
Talked w/ Daniel Higgs on the phone about our proposed gig either Saturday or Sunday (probably).
Finished reading Greg Bear's <u>Darwin's Radio</u> either Saturday or Sunday (probably).

Monday, August 22nd, 2005EV

Bernard called from Baltimore to talk about the recent P-Burgh police brutality, etc..
Got a great package from Germ!
etta returned safely from Red Onion prison & we had breakfast together.
Sent off the VD-RADIO package to Pippi.
Saw Mikey @ Paul's CDs.
Saw Margaret outside in Bloomfield & she seems much better.
Listened to the CDs that Germ sent, read some of the Preparation X 7 zine of Skip's that she sent,

& watched the Quasi DVD that she sent.

Tuesday, August 23rd, 2005EV

Finished editing & burned the "Testes-3 Library C (abridged)" CD & started working on "Library F".

Wednesday, August 24th, 2005EV

Finished recording & burning both the unedited & the edited "Testes-3 Library F".
FINALLY finished reading David Foster Wallace's Everything and More.
Checked out the Best of Aurora Picture Show - Volume 2 DVD that Germ sent me & liked some of it alot.

Thursday, August 25th, 2005EV

Went to look by bike at another house (211 Sutton St) in Fine View & rejected it.
Cleared up some e-mail confusion w/ Germ.
Had a diplomatic discussion w/ Michael.
Worked on "Testes-3 Library E" some more.
Had fun jabbering out front w/ the nieghbors & their friends.

Friday, August 26th, 2005EV

Got the last of the bks that I ordered on-line in the mail today:
>Giordano Bruno's <u>Cause, Principle, and Unity and Essays on Magic</u>.

etta called & made birthday plans w/ me.
Watched <u>The Club</u> DVD that Germ sent me. Doing so has proved (as if I didn't already 'know')
>that I have extraordinary powers of

endurance & dedication.

Saturday, August 27th, 2005EV

Hung out w/ Michael Pestel a little.
Watched <u>Night of the Dawn of the Day of the Return of the Flesheating, Hellbound,</u>
>Subhumanoid Living Dead PART 2 - wch

wasn't particularly funny but at least I got it over w/!

Sunday, August 28th, 2005EV

Hung out w/ Margaret a little - she seems pretty good.
Got e-mails from Jeanine AND Julie AND Germaine!

Time to check out another movie - Robert Altman's <u>Quintet</u> tonight (wch I liked alot).

Monday, August 29th, 2005EV

"It dreamed to me" (to quote the subtitled translation of Kaspar Hauser in the Herzog film) that I had been selected for a project for wch I'd gone to 'the Netherlands' to collaborate w/ some famous people that included David Bowie & Joe Silva? I think maybe we were going to use vacuum cleaner sounds as part of it? I was honored by this at 1st until I realized that the other people picked were all very young art student types. I was in a skyscraper & had possibly just had an operation the day before. I was impatiently waiting for something to happen & wanted to go outside to shoot an upside-down shot of another skyscraper. Then etta was there too & she was impatient to get back to her prison work.

[It's been hard to be positive these past few days! BUT, now I can use this POSITIVE diary as an excuse to sneak in some kvetching & still give it a positive spin! Friday, the pedal fell of my main bike & I cdn't fix it. I had to half-ride, half-walk it for miles. I started using my back-up bike but 1st I had to fix its brakes. Either Friday or Saturday, pains in the small of my back started feeling serious & leading me to think that I might have prostate cancer. The pain seems to be increasing every day & is making functioning difficult. Of course, I don't have health insurance or the money to see a doctor - AND I'm not sure I'd want to anyway. I have to die sooner or later & now might be as good a time as ever given that no-one's in love w/ me & no-one's dependent on me & it's pretty clear that my life is probably not going to get any better. Either Friday or Saturday, the downstairs computer, wch I use as my main audio recorder, ceased to work for recording anymore & the printer there stopped feeding the paper - both of these things stopped the TESTES-3 mega-project I was at the beginning of. Saturday night I went to go look at a house & the key didn't work so I cdn't get inside. Then the ATM ate my bank-card so I cdn't get any money out, some time was wasted & I didn't end up going to my entertainment for the nite. I called the bank's emergency # & asked them to stop the card so that no-one cd use it fraudulently. Sunday my back-up bike tube broke & I cdn't fix that so I ended up walking the bike about 5 miles. Then today I had to ride/walk bike #1 in the pouring rain to the bank a coupla miles away to find out that my card had been totally stopped & that I'd have to get a new one & then another mile or so to the bike repair shop to take care of all that mess. SO, how can I make all that positive? Well.. I'll ignore the possibility of prostate cancer for the moment! Maybe it'll give my life some new zest! (Just kidding?!) What I realised while I was dealing w/ the bank & the bike today was that, unlike most of my life, I actually had the money to do these things. In the past, such situations wd've quite possibly resulted in some extremely desperate conditions. I wdn't've even HAD a bike - OR a bank acct. I wd've more likely not had enuf money to buy food (Today I went out to eat) or to take the bus (If I'd had a bike I certainly wdn't've had any money for fixing it), I wd've probably been in the midst of some extremely emotionally charged situation that wd've been keeping me seriously borderline suicidal & these problems wd've increased the aggravation & made dealing w/ life even more difficult. If I were still living in Baltimore there wd've been predators following me & theratening me on a daily basis. Walk a bike in Baltimore? Yeah, & risk getting your head clubbed so someone cd steal it. That sort of thing. At least these days when I realize my shaving cream is running out I can actually afford to get some! It might not seem like much, but in the past even such a little thing wd've meant shaving w/ soapy water for a coupla wks before I cd spare a measley dollar. Looking back on my life & seeing that the majority of it has been spent in grinding hand-to-mouth maddening poverty, these recent problems (except the possibility of prostate cancer - wch killed Frank Zappa at my age & led to Timothy Leary's assisted suicide) are extremely trivial in contrast. It cd be (& often has been) much MUCH worse. At least I'm not in Rashid's situation, in prison for life w/ his eye-sight failing him, making it more difficult for him to make those meticulous drawings that he can use as an outlet for & articulate expression of his anger w/ this racist, classist society.]

Got to send off a big package to Germ & Skip today.
Got 3 DVDs & some other things in the mail

today from Germ! Love ya Germ!
Got to fix both my bikes for not too much money.
Watched Andrzej Zulawski's Szamanka.
Had an e-mail chat w/ Germ.

Tuesday, August 30th, 2005EV

Bruce Stater sent me a bk of his that he dedicated to me! Love ya Bruce!
Added 6 more movies to my collection in anticipation of etta watching something w/ me on my birthday.
FINALLY finished editing & burning the Testes-3 Library E CDs after having to reset up the relevant equipment upstairs.
Finished reading the last of the 3 "Preparation X"s Germ sent me.
Didn't drink alcohol.
Watched the A/V Geeks Those Naughty Commies DVD that Germ sent me.

Wednesday, August 31st, 2005EV

Julie's back!
Got a birthday present check from my mom.
etta came by & hung out. We watched Woody Allen's The Purple Rose of Cairo.
Went to etta & The Hollow Sisters' performance at The Pittsburgh Deli Company. It was fun.

Came home drunk & recklessly pro/con-fessed my love (via e-mail) to Germ!
    Quite a hot exchange of e-mails followed! This is both exhilirating & frightening!!!!!

Thursday, September 1st, 2005EV

More intensive e-mailing w/ Germ.
Finished entering the last of Testes-3 Reel C-F into the computer.
Went out to lunch, etc, w/ Julie. Made plans w/ her for tomorrow.
Watched <u>Ed Wood - Look Back In Angora</u>.
Finished editing & burning the Testes-3 Library D (abridged) CDs.
Didn't drink any alcohol.
Transferred Testes-3 Reel G1.

Friday, September 2nd, 2005EV

Got up early & rode bikes on the North Side w/ Julie - checking out yet another house in Fine View, etc..
Went kayaking w/ Julie.
etta cleaned my kitchen sink for my birthday! Bless 'er!
Kim left a message for me offering to take me out to the movies for my birthday to see Terry Gilliam's

<u>The Brothers Grimm</u>.
Went to Michael's latest performance at the Miller Gallery at CMU.
Went out to eat (AGAIN!).
Went to the party at the Big House & didn't drink any alcohol there. But I DID get into alotof interesting   conversations w/ Tait's twin brother & Soren & Alberto &, most importantly, w/ Gretchen who I   was coincidentally seeing for the 3rd day in a row. At least a few people told me, quite   unexpectedly, that I was important to them somehow or another - wch made me feel good! Kenny even told me he planned to give me a clarinet! Came home to more e-mails from the beloved GERM.

<u>Saturday, September 3rd, 2005EV</u>

Finished reading Upton Sinclair's GREAT <u>The Jungle</u> today.
Got ANOTHER package from Germ w/ 2 Severed Heads CDs & other stuff.
Picked up DVD copies of <u>A Chinese Ghost Story</u> II & III.
Read MORE e-mails from Germ & replied.
Took the dive & called Gretchen & invited her to Sean & Breen's party tonight. At 1st she seemed pleased   & sd YES but THEN, when I called her back & left her my phone # & more explicit directions she   called back & sd she'd probably stay home where it's peaceful.
Oh well! It was worth a try. She   DID

propose that we collaborate but we went no further w/ that.

Sunday, September 4th, 2005EV

Whew! What a day this has been! It seems like it's been a long time since I've been able to be positive
    about my birthday but today's been a particularly good one.
Suzie had left a message on my answering machine & sent me an e-mail wishing me Happy Birthday.
I talked w/ Michael Evans on the phone & we got some of our communication problems straightened out
    so now it'll be easier for me to set up our proposed gig. Maybe the possibility of the gig & the   possibility of a drum set being needed will prompt me to rebuild mine.
Mark & Julie took me out to eat at the Orient Kitchen (is that what it's called?) - wch is fairly close to here   but I'd never been there. The food was good & I had fun.
Then I went to Paul's CDs & etta & I bought me a slew of great new music for me to listen to.
I ran into several people I knew at Paul's & they all wished me HB.
When I got home there was a very unexpected & VERY welcome message from Gretchen on the answering
    machine. This led to my calling her & our having a short conversation. The feeling that

this might
> lead to something more substantial is
still there.
I worked on the Testes-3 project more. I'm on Library G now.
etta brought home some Thai food & we watched <u>A Chinese Ghost Story II</u> wch was alotof fun.
Jeanine & I talked on the phone for about an hr & a half.
Didn't drink alcohol.

Monday, September 5th, 2005EV

Joe Abeln called to wish me Happy Birthday.
I finally talked w/ GERM! This's still very open-ended but it seems that there's a possible strong future here.
Didn't drink alcohol.

Tuesday, September 6th, 2005EV

Started the new job & the people were nice.
Met Julie & Mark at the Rock Room for food & drink.

Wednesday, September 7th, 2005EV

The plethora of Germ e-mails make the day go by.

Thursday, September 8th, 2005EV

Kim took me to Terry Gilliam's The Brothers Grimm for my birthday.

Friday, September 9th, 2005EV

Rode bikes w/ Julie to the North Side & took her to the Mattress Factory & the Warhol.
THEN we went to a free booze party at the Oakland Library!!
Stopped by Kalie's where there was a surprise birthday party for her.
THEN I went to Babs's place to cheer her up.
Went to Gordon's birthday party in Lawrenceville.
Stopped by Lisa's place to tell her that there was a party of friendly people nearby.
Went to the party at Lorraine's for Benny & Aurelia & got Jo(e)y to stay at my place to keep him out of trouble.
A slew of e-mails from Germ have once again convinced me (like I need more?) that something great is going on here. I finally extended an invitation to her for her to live w/ me & she seems to've accepted.

Saturday, September 10th, 2005EV

Germ sent me TWENTY-THREE emails in 19 hrs! Omigoodness!!
Kelly came by! He evacuated from New Orleans in time.
I got up to Library H1 in the Testes-3 project.
Didn't drink alcohol.

Sunday, September 11th, 2005EV

I made the last of my USIC vaudeos for Germ today. I'll send her a package tomorrow.
I finished reading Bruce's bk present to me today: <u>the language of angels: a noemorphoetic codex</u>.
Germ referred to us as a "couple" (by implication). Our correspondence is very relaxed & loving.
Had a long phone conversation w/ etta about a possible collaboration re murder & moral dillemmas of   prison activists.
Didn't drink alcohol.

Monday, September 12th, 2005EV

Hung out w/ Julie while running errands - wch included sending off a big package to Germ &

Skip.
Made 11 new copies of both volumes of Piano Illiterature.
Got some more music from Paul's - including another John Fahey CD.
Watched Kafka w/ Mark & Julie. Enjoyed it (even though the 'anarchists' were somewhat unconvincing).

Tuesday, September 13th, 2005EV

Encountered Kelly en route to work.
Message on answering machine from Kelly re working on a new movie.
Talked w/ Germ on the phone AGAIN.
Hung out w/ Julie & Mark at the Rock Room.
Sent an email to Air Guitar Magazine.

Wednesday, September 14th, 2005EV

Free pizza at work today.
Learned that the Three Rivers Film Festival IS planning to screen Story of a Fructiferous Society!
    THANK YOU GEORGE DAVIS!
Kelly & April came by & hooked me up w/ free food,
Brainstormed on the new collaborative movie at Morgan's house. I'm to be the HAM
    (Holy Ascended Master) in the Bladder Control Religion.

As Julie pointed out last nite, all I have to do for an entry in this is remark that I communicated w/ Germ   today. True, so true.
Watched the 1st part of the BBC's The Power of Nightmares about the use of the 'threat of terrorism' for
    the consolidation of fundamentalist power.

Thursday, September 15th, 2005EV

Lisa Stolarski called & Invited me out.
April & Kelly came by to see Story of a Fructiferous Society & to shoot a scene or 2 on the new movie.
Courtney called & invited me to a birthday party for Margaret.
Watched the 2nd part of the BBC's The Power of Nightmares.

Friday, September 16th, 2005EV

Finished the Frick job today & got the repros of most of the drawings for my personal collection.
Finished watching The Power of Nightmares.
Talked w/ Germ for an hr & a half.
Watched the Private SNAFU cartoons.

Saturday, September 17th, 2005EV

Got a SLEW of emails from GERM - ONE OF WCH
BORDERED ON AN IMPLIED MARRIAGE
PROPOSAL!!!!!!
      Such an entry deserves to be repeated!
Got a SLEW of emails from GERM - ONE OF WCH
BORDERED ON AN IMPLIED MARRIAGE
PROPOSAL!!!!!!
      Such an entry deserves to be repeated!
Had a brief visit from Daryl Fleming & might
collaborate w/ him again.
Picked up an early Cronenberg I THOUGHT I
hadn't seen: <u>They Came From Within</u> (it turned
out to be <u>Shivers</u> + 12 Flash Gordon
episodes (wch I used to enjoy watching on late-
nite tv as a teenager) + the disinformation DVD
set.
Greg loaned me a movie called <u>The Good Fight</u>.
Scored some free food at the Warhol.
Met a nice electro-mechincal repairman who
might fix my echoplex, etc..
Carlin invited me to her birthday party tomorrow.
SHEESH! the marriage-related emails have been
passing hot & heavy! (one exclamation mark
represents
      infinity or sumpin')
How can I end such a day's entries?!

<u>Sunday, September 18th, 2005EV</u>

Talked w/ Germ AGAIN!
Went to Carlin's birthday party & had fun.
Babs thanked me for being such a good friend.
Julie & I said how much we love each each other.

Monday, September 19th, 2005EV

Didn't have to work today.
Suzie emailed me.
Wrote to Jen Roth about some confusion in connection w/ the brain scan project & rc'vd a clarification.
Made 2 Triple-S Variety Show tapes for Germ.
Started work on IMP ACTIVISM 7 - especially the beginning.
Jona Pelovska called me from Toronto & we talked for over an hr!
Loaded in the last part of Testes-3 Library H & burned a CD of it.
Continued my Flash Gordon serial entertainment.

Tuesday, September 20th, 2005EV

Mailed off a <u>Story of a Fructiferous Society</u> DVD to Cathy Cook @ UMBC.
Mailed off CDs to Germ's friend Tommy in Richmond for radio play.
Started on Testes-3 Library I & burned the I1 CD.
Watched movies w/ Julie & Mark: <u>A Letter to Mary Ann</u> (WHEW!) & Jonathan Demme's <u>The Agronomist</u>
  (wch was great & wch I've added to my favorite films by other people list).
Was, AS ALWAYS, very moved by correspondence w/ Germaine.

Found some VD-RADIO materials relevant to Pippi & emailed him re same.

Wednesday, September 21st, 2005EV

Finished watching the last of <u>A Letter to Mary Ann</u>.
Wrote more heartfelt emails to Germ.
Went out w/ Julie & she shot some photos of my math tattoo & related stuff for her photography class
        - then we went out to eat at the Spice Cafe where I'd never eaten before.
Worked on Testes-3 Library I2.
Had a long phone conversation w/ Doug Retzler.
Met etta's political activist friend, Tom Big Warrior.

Thursday, September 22nd, 2005EV

Wrote a long email to Germ.
Copied my Mosolov retrospective tape for Germ.
Made plans w/ Cerrina for next Monday.
Worked on trying to arrange the Virgo Party.
Got a collage as a birthday present from Suzie.
Got a $50 check from the Lahns as a birthday present.
Shot some scenes for the still-unnamed colaborative movie at the abdandoned Brereton house.
Went w/ Julie to the Frick opening & then to the

BBT.

Friday, September 23rd, 2005EV

Talked w/ Julie on the phone.
Kevin Hicks called in support of the Virgo Party.
Worked on Testes-3 Library I2 & completed editing it.
Crossed paths w/ Carlin & Josh on the streets & enjoyed talking w/ them.
TALKED W/ GERM ON THE PHONE FOR 3&1/2 HRS!!!!!
& then got off the phone w/ her & emailed her - wch she'd already done to me! What NUTS!
Didn't drink alcohol.

Saturday, September 24th, 2005EV

Finished Testes-3 Library I (abridged) & burned it to a CD.
Edited together a crude "VD-RADIO / Alan Fay" audio piece.
Recorded Testes-3 Library J & burned the CD.
Didn't drink alcohol.

Sunday, September 25th, 2005EV

Finished Testes-3 Libraries J1 & J2 & burned them to CDs.

Copied 2 political documentaries for Germ.
Recorded parts of Chapter 8, "Rock Men", &
subsequent relevant parts of the Flash Gordon
serial entitled   "Space Soldiers Conquer the
Universe" so I can reverse it to hear what the
Rock Men are saying   backwards.
Didn't drink alcohol.

Monday, September 26th, 2005EV

Had a lucid dream where I was trying to ride a
bike w/o there being one underneath me. I
decided it was   easier to do the breast-stroke in
mid-air instead but I wasn't satisfied w/ that &
wanted to go thru   the bike-riding motions
& hover off the ground at the appropriate height
& move at the   appropriate speed.
Worked more on the "Military Backward Masking
in Rock Videos" project that's growing out of the
                backwards Flash Gordon
material.
Booked the flight to Toronto for October 14th
gig.
Went out to eat w/ Cerrina & talked w/ her for
awhile.
Mark came by for our now wkly movie nite. We
watched <u>Ned Kelly</u> (the more recent version w/o
Mick   Jaeger) & we got drunk.
Germ called me around 2AM 'cause she was
worried about me & she cheered me up.

Tuesday, September 27th,

2005EV

Mom & Pop came to visit from Baltimore & brought fresh towels & sheets & toilet-paper & the like & took me out to eat.
Worked on Testes-3 Library J2 some more.
Finished the last episode of the Flash Gordon serial.
Didn't drink alcohol.

Wednesday, September 28th, 2005EV

Learned things from my stepdad about chestnuts.
Got taken out to eat by my mom & stepdad.
Got together w/ Kelly & downloaded more footage for our project.
Got an email from Julie (currently in Baltimore) about her missing me.
Dumped Testes-3 Library J3 into the computer & made a CD from it.
Watched Film as a Subversive Art about Amos Vogel & Cinema 16 wch I thoroughly enjoyed.
Finished editing Testes-3 Library J (abridged) & burned it to CD.

Thursday, September 29th, 2005EV

Worked on the still more or less untitled collaboarative movie that I'm sometimes calling The Discontinuous Universe for 5 hrs w/

Kelly, Dan, Von, & Matthu.
Dumped Testes-3 Library K1 into the computer & burned a CD copy.
Watched <u>The Good Fight</u> again (hadn't seen it for 2 decades?) & was VERY moved.

Friday, September 30th, 2005EV

Got a copy of Walerian Borowczyk's <u>The Beast</u>!
Margaret left a message expressing interest in the Virgo Party.
Got to talk w/ Germaine for a few minutes.
Watched Herzog's INCREDIBLE 1998 <u>Little Dieter Needs To Fly</u>.
etta & I had a substantial talk.

Saturday, October 1st, 2005EV

Got 2 Morton Subotnick DVDs & I particularly enjoyed the interviews w/ him.
Julie's been writing me pretty regularly since she's been in Baltimore.
etta came by & watched a little of <u>A Chinese Ghost Story III</u>.

Sunday, October 2nd, 2005EV

Watched the Xenakis <u>La Legende D'Eer</u> DVD wch has a stupid critic statement re anarchy that I'll

probably   use in "Imagine Utopias".
Picked up the complete Peter Jackson <u>Lord of the Rings</u> set of DVDs & the Wes Craven produced <u>They</u>.
Michael Pestel was passing thru town & came by to witness <u>Story of a Fructiferous Society</u>.
Finished watching <u>A Chinese Ghost Story III</u>.

Monday, October 3rd, 2005EV

I finally started pursuing getting a dental appointment.
I finally started pursuing getting a title search & title insurance (I'm waiting for word from the FL people).
I finally checked a bit more on the 3033 Brereton house.
Suzie called! AND GAVE ME A TAROT READING wch was basically all about the situation w/ Germaine.
Corresponded somewhat w/ David Rothenberg about Whales & Music.
Michael & I went out to eat at the usual Thai place & then watched a Subotnick & a Xenakis DVD.
Talked w/ Debs about the Virgo Party wch I've set for Tuesday, October 11th.
Watched <u>They</u>.
Recorded & burned a CD of Testes-3 Library K3.

Tuesday, October 4th, 2005EV

Germ sent me a photo of herself! (Duly printed out in multiple copies)
Finished watching the Subotnick Volume 1 DVD.
Went to the Rock Room w/ Kim.
Called people re the Virgo Party now scheduled at my house for next Tuesday @ 9PM.
Finished editing Testes-3 Library K (abridged) & burned it to CD.
Dumped Testes-3 Library L1 into the computer & burned it to CD.
Watched Paul Leni's 1927 <u>The Cat and the Canary</u>.

[Have been thinking today about how it'll be interesting to see how what I choose to include here changes as I progress thru this. As I glimpsed very superficially thru past entries, I realized that I didn't mention something that I wd've mentioned before: viz: that my bike chain broke & that as soon as I got home, next-door neighbor Dave was sitting outside & immediately offered to fix it - wch he proceeded to do w/in a matter of minutes! This OBVIOUSLY deserves mention but I've gotten back into the habit of taking for granted certain types of good things - such as that I can still afford to eat out every day, that I have time to read every day, that I have time to listen to music every day (right now it's Feldman's String Quartet 2 performed by the Flux Quartet - GREAT!, ABSOLUTELY GREAT! - & I have the score to it thanks to Ben Opie! Love ya Ben, you great musician, you!), etc.. Basically, I'm probably falling into a routine of automatically slotting some things as positive & neglecting others: ANYTHING HAVING TO DO W/

GERM: GOOD; socializing w/ friends: good; working on projects: good; watching a movie at the end of the day: good (usually), etc.. AND IT IS ALL GOOD! But there's so much more! I haven't really had anything 'bad' happen to me in what seems like a very long time! What a stark contrast to MOST of my life in Baltimore!]

Realized that this love affair w/ Germaine has only been going on for a little over a month! Amazing!!
Talked w/ Germaine on the phone for a long time. & then SOME MORE after we got off the phone for a   while to enable us to give our ears a rest, etc.. Didn't get off the phone 'til 6:45AM!!!!!

Wednesday, October 5th, 2005EV

Germaine made a forthright admission via email that she'd previously avoided.
Worked w/ April & Michael on the "Struggle for the P'Olo Club" scenes.
Finally watched Borowczyk's The Beast w/ April, Mark, & Julie.

Thursday, October 6th, 2005EV

Greg gave me a copy of Crossroads: Avant-garde film in Pittsburgh in the 1970s by Robert A. Haller.

Neely wrote me saying that I might be able to lecture at Wesleyan.
Worked on the "30 4 5 + 97.9" restructuring (version 3).
Talked w/ Germ! (LOVE YA!)

Friday, October 7th, 2005EV

Hung out w/ Julie.
Mailed off packages to David Rothenberg & Johnnny Evans.
Attended the A A Bronson (of General Idea) power point presentation at the Warhol Museum & gave him   some presents.
Went out w/ Mark & Julie to Ed-Um's opening & to Duke's.
TALKED W/ GERMAINE AGAIN ON THE PHONE!!

Saturday, October 8th, 2005EV

Went to the Quiet Storm for their 4th anniversary & to hear Pimps Up Hoedown & talked w/ alotof nice   people - including Lorraine the dental student.

Sunday, October 9th, 2005EV

Made a good interview vaudeo w/ Thomas Silva - the Warhol guard who was a sailor on the aircraft carrier   that took Admiral Byrd's B-25 for launch-off for dropping supplies for Little

America in 1946.
Finished the 3rd version of the "30 4 5 + 97.9" lecture CD.
Went over to Mark & Julie's & watched "One Flew Over the Cuckoo's Nest".
TALKED W/ GERMAINE.

Monday, October 10th, 2005EV

Got my "Barber's Paradox" haircut from Julie.
Made a good interview vaudeo w/ Katie Doody about her piss & shit related extravaganzas.
Talked w/ Lorraine about setting a time for tooth-care.
Got Fabio's images for the Nov 19 gig flier.
Watched Scanner Cop.

Tuesday, October 11th, 2005EV

Finally pulled off the VIRGOS ONLY Party & it was predictably absurd & lots of fun. There were 14 attendees in addition to myself: Carlin Christy, Aurelia Friedland, Benny Parsons, Margaret Campbell, Debs Levine, Ron Douglas, Eric Fleischauer, John Allen Gibel, Kevin Hicks, Kalie Pierce, Mitchell Kulkin, & Mikey Seamans attended of those invited & 2 additonal Virgos were brought: KC Milliken & Jacob Toth. Dan Webb, Adam Abrams, Gordon Nelson, & Oodie didn't attend. This led to a Virgo database & a great excess of beer in my

fridge!
Talked w/ GERM for about 2 hrs!

Wednesday, October 12th, 2005EV

Talked w/ Julie on the phone.
Got David Rothenberg's bk <u>Why Birds Sing</u> in the mail!
Shot a substantial amt of mannequin & doll re-enactments of Katie's incontinence stories for "Discontinuous Universe".
Bought a very nice mandolin for only $75!
Wrote to Elsewhere & proposed a movie-making project there for May, 2006.
Didn't drink alcohol.

Thursday, October 13th, 2005EV

Julie came by & touched up my haircut.
Got a Vermin Supreme DVD in the mail for IMP ACTIVISM purposes.
Got an email from David Rothenberg proposing that I participate in a whales & music CD project.
Started preparing for Toronto trip.
Helped etta w/ her murder-related puppet play sound.
Worked more on "Discontinuous Universe" scans & texts, etc..
Talked to Germaine!
Got a positive reply from Elsewhere.
Didn't drink alcohol.

Friday, October 14th, 2005EV

Was flown to Toronto by Pleasure Dome to screen "Story of a Fructiferous Society" as part of "SoundPlay".
Met my host, Linda Feesey who turned out to be interesting.
Screened "Story.." & had fun w/ the vaudience afterward. Rubber-stamped paper for them so they cd have "stills" from the movie.
Saw Jubal & John Porter & Martin Heath & Bill Satan & Sherri & Armin Kink again & met some new folks like Sarah Peebles.
Went out drinking w/ Bill, Sherri, & Armino & had lively discussions.

Saturday, October 15th, 2005EV

Got some good books.
JONA called me at Linda's!
Attended the SoundPlay festival & enjoyed the Metamkine performance.
Went out to a bar afterward w/ fest people & went w/ 2 new friends, John & Adam, to an "anarchist frat party".

Sunday, October 16th, 2005EV

Wandered around Toronto & eventually talked w/ the Metamkine guys some more at their workshop.
Met Martin at Cinecycle & went to his friend Janet's studio where I got some special clothes. Back at Cinecycle, Jubal & Josh of Fame Fame + John Porter & Martin & Janet & I all hung out & drank
& watched Starevitch's "The Mascot" followed by Martin's found footage feature on the history of rock and roll called "Son of Tutti Frutti" followed by 2 super-8 shorts of Martin's & 6 of John's - all of wch I thoroughly liked. It was a great nite!
Talked w/ Germ late after I got back to Linda & Jonathan's.

Monday, October 17th, 2005EV

Got some more good books & headed home from Toronto.
Talked w/ Lorraine the dental student over the phone & made an appointment for dental work. Solidified the 3 Rivers Film festival dates.
Listened to the Sarah Peebles CDs & watched the John & Adam DVD that I got in Toronto. Watched the Hollywood-esque <u>The Anarchist Cookbook</u> wch had its 'anarchist' hero become an FBI informer who hooks up w/ an S&M Republican girl. It was good to see what kind of warp such a movie wd make of such a subject. I enjoyed it even though the treatment was the usual ball of silly inaccuracies: anarchists mainly eating meat from fast food

places? Wha?!

Tuesday, October 18th, 2005EV

Julie came by & hung out a bit.
Watched <u>Deadful Melody</u> w/ Julie & Mark.

Wednesday, October 19th, 2005EV

Julie & I went out & looked at 2 houses for sale & went thrift store shopping etc.. I got a bunch of some   snazzy shirts & a bath-robe & some videos & a DVD & some strange glasses/bottles, etc..
Got a HUGE package from Germaine today that's so full of goodies that I've barely begun to process it all.
Bret McCabe's friendly review of "Story of a Fructiferous Society" appeared in the Baltimore City Paper.
Jesse McLean invited me over to Filmmakers for a special screening.
Talked w/ the GERM. Goofball.

Thursday, October 20th, 2005EV

Got a CD from Carrie Shull.
Finally got Sue Abramson's <u>Extended Frames</u> photography book w/ the CoAccident fotos!

Mailed a package to David Rothenberg.
Julie & I ran errands together & went to <u>Radio Alice</u> screening.
Opened up a gmail email acct.

<u>Friday, October 21st, 2005EV</u>

Got a substantial amt of photocopying done that I'd put off for YEARS.
Vaudeoed etta & friends' <u>The Hardest Question Ever</u> puppet show at The Seventh Annual Black Sheep   Puppet Festival.

<u>Saturday, October 22nd, 2005EV</u>

Ok, as is sometimes the case here, the day wasn't too promising on the "positive" end: I got a flat riding   my bike to work in the cold rain, I fixed it in the rain, I got ANOTHER flat riding home from work in   the rain, I tried to fix that one & failed. FORTUNATELY, when I still had 2 miles to walk in the cold   rain pushing my bike Katie Doody stopped & offered a ride. Thank you, Katie!!
Had a LONG conversation w/ Germaine about things like my relationship w/ the Church of the SubGenius.

<u>Sunday, October 23rd, 2005EV</u>

Well! Yesterday I got YET ANOTHER FLAT in the rain so I didn't mention that before because I didn't want to strain TOO MUCH to squeeze something positive out of it but today I got a 4TH FLAT IN 24 HRS & had a stranger offer me a ride while I was trying to fix it yet again! SO, THAT was POSITIVE.

Then I succeeded in fixing it enuf so it didn't get a flat on the way home from work. Dumped Thomas Silva's interview & <u>The Hardest Question Ever</u> into the computer & burned DVDs from them to give to the relevant people. Watched the 1st Wonder Showzen program on the DVD that Germ sent me. Pretty damn funny. GERM called me to wish me an early good nite! LOVE YOU GERM!!
Watched <u>Monty Python & the Holy Grail</u> either for the 1st time (hard to believe) or after such a long interval that I'd forgotten it. Thought it was GREAT! Totally enjoyed it.

<u>Monday, October 24th, 2005EV</u>

Julie called. She's back from B-More. Thank the holy ceiling light!
Got DSL & otherwise took care of many quasi-banal odds & ends.
Made a vaudeo for Greg.
Wrote "Barber's Paradox Haircut" for use in the Haircut Paradox movie.
Watched the 2nd Wonder Showzen program.
Watched Jackie Chan's <u>Rumble in the Bronx</u>.
Had a long late-nite conversation w/Germaine.

Tuesday, October 25th, 2005EV

Brian Gentry emailed me.
I got an offer to buy a copy of <u>Homeless Movies</u> from a place in Rochester.
Matt Teichman brought by Bruce Conner video comp w/ 10 movies for me to watch - wch I did, making notes.
Skizz wrote to me w/ interview questions.

Wednesday, October 26th, 2005EV

Finally shot the going-to-the-Post-Office scene for the Book 'Em documentary.
Worked on package for Martin Heath.
Watched the latest Vermin Supreme DVD - WONDERFUL! & the 3rd & 4th Wonder Showzen episodes
    - also GREAT! - w/ Julie & Mark - who laughed alot.
Replaced ink cartridges in printer.
Was pleasantly surprised to see that Mary Woronov, Candy Darling, & Ondine were in the cast of <u>Silent Night, Bloody Night</u>.

Thursday, October 27th, 2005EV

Mailed package to Martin.

Picked up a bk on all of Guy Debord's films & a DVD of <u>Capturing the Friedmans</u> & a DVD of Bill Morrison & Michael Gordon's <u>Decasia</u>.
Fixed BOTH of my bikes.
Finished 20 more "pond(er)" packages.
Witnessed <u>Decasia</u> & listened to the related interview.
Had a 3 hr late nite phone conversation w/ Germaine.

Friday, October 28th, 2005EV

Went to a party at the Big House as "The Guy Who Goes to the Party without a Costume".

Saturday, October 29th, 2005EV

Participated in a GREAT local screening at Jefferson Presents.
Went to one of the best parties I've ever been to in Pittsburgh on Evaline.

Sunday, October 30th, 2005EV

Went to the Mattress Factory for their small press "Swap Meet" & met Jacob of Paper Rad & traded.
Talked briefly w/ Germaine.
etta came by & we watched the beginning of <u>The</u>

Lord of the Rings together.

Monday, October 31st, 2005EV

Julie gave me a cabinet she dumpstered.
Met Carol & Rich of the Three Rivers Film Festival & gave them 3 promotional DVDs of "Story..".
Went out to eat w/ Julie at the Orient Kitchen.
Helped Julie make a little money today distributing Three Rivers Film Festival brochures.
Got EVEN MORE used clothes to spice up my wardrobe.
Edited all of Testes-3 Library L1.
etta came by & watched more Fellowship of the Ring.
Talked a little w/ Germaine before we got cut off.

Tuesday, November 1st, 2005EV

Set up my DSL account.
Coincidentally encountered Julie on Herron Avenue.
April came by & I got the last of the "Discontinuous Universe" footage & the P'Olo Club.
Talked very briefly w/ Germaine before we got cut off.
Designed the poster for the November 19th gig.
etta came by & watched more Fellowship of the Ring.

Germ actually went to the trouble of biking to a payphone to call me!

Wednesday, November 2nd, 2005EV

[Often these entries are very cut & dried. Of course, there's far more omitted than included. I rarely mention work since I don't consider my being 'forced' into the capitalist market to be positive. Then again, the workplace is both educational & social &, therefore, positive after all. Also, I read every day & listen to music every day & rarely mention either. I only mention the bks when I finish them & then only if I think the bk was remarkable. At the moment I'm reading at least 5 bks so finishing any one is not necessarily near. As such, this diary gives the false impression of NO reading. I also don't mention movies witnessed that I don't think are somehow exceptional. But, nonetheless, I watch many just for the experience & "recreation" of doing so - horror movies that aren't very original but I still find something interesting in them. Furthermore (interesting word), I go into very little detail most of the time. An entry such as "Ran errands w/ Julie today" doesn't tell much about what fun we might've had talking & such-like things.]

Ran errands w/ Julie today that included checking on car rental prices, copying Nov 19 gig poster materials, & food shopping. Had a fellow named Che Elias offer to publish a bk by me!! He came into the copy shop & talked

w/ me - telling me that he'd liked the movies that I screened last Saturday. We exchanged contact info & I sent him some writing samples by email later on after he emailed me. THANK YOU CHE!!
Julie refreshed by math haircut. THANK YOU JULIE!!
Worked on assembling the Nov 19 gig posters & gave a few away.
Finished reading Cornell Woolrich's <u>I Married a Dead Man</u>.
Didn't drink alcohol.

Thursday, November 3rd, 2005EV

Finished making the posters for the Nov 19 gig.
Rehearsed playing the oboe samples for tomorrow nite's gig.
Worked on my proposed SIX GALLERY PRESS book.

Friday, November 4th, 2005EV

Started repairing my Erector Set in prep for the Nov 19 gig.
Improvised w/ Kevin & Elina at their opening at the Modern Formations Gallery.

Saturday, November 5th, 2005EV

Scanned & updated "Telepathy Receptivity Training" & sent it off to Che as a <u>footnotes</u> chapter.
Attended the <u>X: The Man With The X-Ray Eyes</u> screening w/ Pere Ubu providing an "underscore".

Sunday, November 6th, 2005EV

Talked w/ Germaine twice.

Monday, November 7th, 2005EV

Sent off press releases for Nov 19 gig.
Worked more on repairing & cleaning of Erector Set.
Greg brought by 3 DVDs for me to check out & Alisa gave me a copy of the latest issue of "Xtra Tuf".

Tuesday, November 8th, 2005EV

Worked on Erector Set & played it some more.
FINALLY finished reading Cornell Woolrich's intense <u>Waltz into Darkness</u> wch completes the CW Omnibus.
Sent out announcement to Baltimore Bulk email list re "..Fructiferous.." screening in

MicroCineFest.
Started working on Gnome Samples.
Watched Dusty Nelson's <u>Effects</u>
     & am pleasantly surprised to find Jarry's
<u>Ubu</u> as one of the extras on the DVD!

Wednesday, November 9th, 2005EV

Sent out announcement to Pittsburgh Bulk email
list re "..Fructiferous.." screening in
     Three Rivers Film Festival.
Talked w/ Germaine on the phone.
Worked on updating the FLICKER Press website.
Sorted thru some more material for <u>footnotes</u>.
Didn't drink alcohol.
Talked w/ Germ late at nite.

Thursday, November 10th, 2005EV

Julie gave me a ride to B-More to her mom's
where I managed to get enuf sleep so I cd recoup
from my   cold/flu somewhat.
Didn't drink alcohol.

Friday, November 11th, 2005EV

Attended the 1st series of shorts in the
MicroCinefest - many of wch I liked alot.
Had J.R. Fritsch offer to distribute my records &

advance pd for 5 <u>Usic - √-1</u>s (at $10 apiece).
Screened "Story of a Fructiferous Society" in the
fest - where Skizz was EXTREMELY SUPPORTIVE
          - even to the point of having a stereo
sound system for the 1st time!
Made enuf money at this to cover my expenses
& then some.
Didn't drink alcohol.
Talked w/ Germ in the wee hrs once I got back to
P-Burgh (thanks, once again, to Julie)

Saturday, November 12th, 2005EV

Saw <u>Derailroaded</u>, the Wild Man Fischer
documentary in the Three Rivers Film Festival.
Germaine finished uploading both volumes of
<u>Piano Illiterature</u> to the Internet Archive. GOTTA
LOVE 'ER!!

Sunday, November 13th, 2005EV

Started work on my Annotated Movieography for
<u>footnotes</u>.

Monday, November 14th, 2005EV

Went to the dental school & got an idea of how
much I'll be robbed for minimal care.
Worked on notes to be uploaded re the <u>Piano</u>

Illiterature pieces.
Che Elias from SIX GALLERY PRESS came by & we hung out & got to know each other a little.
Screened Story of a Fructiferous Society at Filmmakers to a small but appreciative audience.
Went out w/ friends to drink afterward.

Tuesday, November 15th, 2005EV

Greg showed me some of the 35mm program that I'd missed last Friday.
Found out that I'll be paid more than I'd expected for the Three Rivers Film Festival screenings.
Worked more on the Piano Illiterature notes.
Shot more vaudeo footage of The Hardest Question Ever.
Watched Stay Free's Illegal Art DVD.
Worked more on transcribing the Surreal Estates interview.

Wednesday, November 16th, 2005EV

Finished typing the Surreal Estates interview.
Worked more on the Annotated Movieography.
Got pd $200 for being in the Three Rivers Film Festival.
Got an adequate write-up in the Pittsburgh City Paper for the upcoming Nov 19 gig that shd attract a   crowd.
Picked up some CDs at Paul's - including another Pierre Bastien & a nice Plunderphonics set.

Got some clamp lamps to replace the broken light in the bedroom.
FINALLY got an email from Germ after a more than 36 hr 'silence'.
Greg agreed to vaudeo Saturday's show.
Redid "booed usic" SOUND timings in prep for Saturday's gig.

Thursday, November 17th, 2005EV

Finished more prep for the Nov 19 gig.
Fabio & Michael arrived & we went to the Hitchcock / Alloy Orchestra Blackmail event wch was GREAT.

Friday, November 18th, 2005EV

Went w/ F&M to the General Idea show at the Warhol.
Went w/ F&M record shopping at Jerry's & picked up an Aeolian Harp LP, an LP w/ an Ornstein orchestral piece, & "Hard Rope & Silken Twine" by the Incredible String Band.

Saturday, November 19th, 2005EV

Pulled off the gig w/ a pretty substantial amt of help from my friends - esp. Julie, Greg, & etta AS USUAL!

Hung out not only w/ M&F but also Daniel & etta.
Both Suzie & Germaine left me phone messages.

Sunday, November 20th, 2005EV

Back to having the house to myself & trying to get my life back in order.
Got a shitload of movies at Eide's today.
Jona called & we had a pleasant chat. She's still proposing that I show my movies in Montréal.
Didn't drink alcohol.
etta came over & we watched the last of The Fellowship of the Ring.

Monday, November 21st, 2005EV

Ran errands that included food shopping.
Germaine sent me a synthesized voice message since she's too hoarse to talk!
Worked substantially on the Proposals section of footnotes.

Tuesday, November 22nd, 2005EV

Cleaned the basement a little in prep for reassembling/reorganizing the percussion.
Edited the Nov 19 mini-discs down to a 120 minute cassette.
Cleaned out extraneous materials on the

computer somewhat.
Edited Julie & Suzie & José's "Dream" movie somewhat.
FINALLY FINISHED READING Giordano Bruno's <u>The Expulsion of the Triumphant Beast</u>!
Dumped Greg's footage from the Nov 19 into the computer in prep for making a short movie from it.
Found a "Tacheles" scene in <u>Hidden Agenda</u> that I can incorporate into <u>IMP ACTIVISM 7</u>.

Wednesday, November 23rd, 2005EV

Worked more on <u>footnotes</u> - including starting to write its intro.
Ate quesadillas at etta's. Thanks etta!
Packaged & started copying 10 Volunteers Collective <u>A Year of Sundays</u> tapes.
Watched Alfred Hitchcock's <u>The Birds</u> & recorded its soundtrack because it has music by
    Remi Gassman & Oskar Sala. Also excerpted from it for audience reaction shots for "history in the making.".

Thursday, November 24th, 2005EV

Finished one phase of my Annotated Movieography.
Andalusia called & invited me to Mary Mac & Jessica's place.
Jona called & talked w/ me for a long time.

Finished copying 10 <u>A Year of Sundays</u> tapes.
Finished the "booed usic" section of "history in the making.".

Friday, November 25th, 2005EV

Went to Kalie & Doug's for post-T-Giving eating & socializing.
Finished "history in the making." - wch is a nice little edit.
Germ told me via phone that she'd be driving to visit w/in a wk.

Saturday, November 26th, 2005EV

Germ called before I went to work.
Made 11 copies of "history in the making.".
Mikey invited me to Jo(e)y's 25th B-day party at Duke's & I went & had some fun.
Witnessed <u>The House on Garibaldi Street</u> - the 1st movie of my planned double feature on the capture of
    Adolph Eichmann. It was interested to read in the credits that it was shot in Spain in 1979 - 3 yrs,
    as I recall, after Franco died.

Sunday, November 27th, 2005EV

Talked w/ Jeanine on the phone.
Slightly redid "history in the making." & burned 2 fresh copies.
etta visited & we checked out the 1st half of Alex Jones' <u>Martial Law</u>.

Monday, November 28th, 2005EV

etta slept over last nite & I had a very interesting dream where I awoke & she was in bed next to me & Margaret got in bed next to her as if that was nothing unusual. This wasn't a sexual thing - it was more like Margaret routinely came by to watch movies or some such or that she lived there & was just happening to fall asleep w/ us because it was convenient. In the dream I got out of bed, I think partially because I was confused by Margaret being there, & I discovered that I was in a mansion about 6 times the size of my actual house. I walked down the steps, I think the electricity may've been off & I may've been carrying a flashlight, & at the bottom where my kitchen usually is & where the back of the house usually is, the house extended further & there was another staircase going down to a front door. An older man was, perhaps, helping someone move into the house & a younger fellow opened an apparent bedroom door off of this staircase & grinned wildly at me - as if he 'understood' what was going on or was

under the influence of a consciousness
expansion substance. I was confused &
was wondering who these people were &
was thinking of asking them what they
were doing in my house. I may've asked
the older man why the electricity was off
& he may've sd something about its
being because of some major experiment
being conducted nearby. I think I
realized from this that I was in a
university neighborhood & speculated
that the experiment had somehow
created a situation where I had crossed
over into a parallel universe. etta came
down from the bedroom & I asked to
look at her face suspecting that she'd
look different but that she'd, somehow,
still be etta. Sure enuf, her face was
much longer than usual & otherwise
different &, as I watched it, it shrunk a
little but was still different from her
usual face.

Went to the dental school this morning & had my
teeth cleaned. Joe was leaving as I
arrived & it was nice to see him.

FINALLY finished reading the Guy Debord
<u>Complete Cinematic Works</u> collection
from Ken Knabb.

Julie's back from B-More & she brought back the
nice cassette deck that her dad gave her
for me to borrow.

Alexi Morrisey came by w/ stickers for the Wake
Up Call project that I contributed to.

Made copies of the Nov 19 2 hr audio K7 for the
participants.

Worked on my Annotated Movieography some

more for <u>footnotes</u>.
Watched the remainder of the Alex Jones movie.
Didn't drink any alcohol.

<u>Tuesday, November 29th, 2005EV</u>

Worked on the Annotated Movieography more.
Fixed my green bike w/ the good brakes.
Went to the Rock Room for cheap food & booze
    & hug out at Kalie & Doug's afterward.
Checked out <u>The Man Who Captured Eichmann</u> -
    in continuation of the double feature
    started Saturday. This one was actually
    shot in Buenos Aires, Argentina.

<u>Wednesday, November 30th, 2005EV</u>

Mailed off packages to Daniel, Fabio, & Michael.
Borrowed some vaudeos from the Warhol.
Talked w/ Julie on the phone about Germaine.
Worked on the Annotated Movieography more.
Mark invited me to see a martial arts movie w/
    me at a friend's place.
Talked w/ Jeanine on the phone - it's her 38th
    birthday.
Witnessed the vaudeo transfer slide show re-
    enactment of Jack Smith's "The Secret
    of Rented Island" based on Ibsen's play
    "Ghosts". This prompted me to dig up a
    copy of the original in my library to read
    it so I can have more of a clue about

what's going on in the Smith.
Didn't drink any alcohol - making a total of 7 days w/o alcohol this mnth.

Thursday, December 1st, 2005EV

Suzie called me!
Julie treated me to lunch at the newly reopened café at Filmmakers - run by Camera Dave!
Worked on more scans for footnotes.
Got reconciled w/ Germ. [As usual, the oddity of this POSITIVE DIARY is that my having problems is left out - therefore, when Germaine & I are "reconciled" it's positive but out of context.]
Watched the 1st 3 movies of the A/V Geeks "Science" DVD - the last part watched being from the Stanley Milgram "Obedience to Authority" experiment. As usual, a movie possibility pops into my head - a simple re-edit of the Milgram material w/ the 2 Eichmann movies.
Sent Germaine a Wake Up Call message.

Friday, December 2nd, 2005EV

Talked w/ Germaine twice!
Finished scanning all the Reactionary Muddle America papers.
Talked w/ Julie on the phone.

Listened to all my Cream records & felt
rock'n'roll adrenaline rush.
Kim invited me out to the 1st Friday stuff.
Suzie called me twice!
Sent out more Wake Up calls.
Dumped in 2 more versions of "The Hardest
Question Ever" into its computer file.
Watched "Living in a Reversed World" - the last
movie on the A/V Geeks <u>Science</u> DVD.
Sarah called me!
Watched Bruce Lee's <u>Fists of Fury</u>.

<u>Saturday, December 3rd, 2005EV</u>

Sewed my velcro sweatshirt.
Had dinner at etta's.
Converted & laboriously altered 138 frames of
    <u>Story of a Fructiferous Society</u> for
    <u>footnotes</u>.
Talked w/ Julie on the phone.
Started listening to all my old Musicworks tapes.
Didn't drink alcohol.

<u>Sunday, December 4th, 2005EV</u>

Continued listening to all my old Musicworks
    tapes. Was glad to hear a whole side of
    bpNichol.
Watched Bruce Lee's <u>The Chinese Connection</u>
    during downtime at work today. The
    weirdest thing about it was a scene

where it seemed to imply that Lee cd
tell that a guy was Japanese by his
nipples?!
Talked w/ Germaine in Cleveland.
Worked on <u>footnotes</u> a little.

Monday, December 5th, 2005EV

[Once again, it's interesting to me to note what I
consider to be an appropriate entry for
this POSITIVE Diary. Today, I can still
remember a dream somewhat & I want
to describe it here & I'm considering
what criteria a dream must meet to be
"positive". The thing is that dreams are
invariably interesting to me &, therefore,
more or less always positive. I reckon I
haven't decided yet whether all
nightmares are then positive for that
reason.]

Dreamt this morning as if I were an observer
(wch seems to be often the case). As
such, I had a detached consciousness
that was trying to interpret what I was
seeing. There was a fairly large group of
people in KKK-like outfits on an "outing
in the country". They were traveling in
multiple vehicles - probably including
buses, possible school buses. It was
warm outside, the area where they were
disembarking from the vehicles was
partially wooded, partially open, & the
road(s) leading to it was a/were country
road(s) - probably paved but small. The

thing about this description is that I was conscious w/in the dream of making interpretive decisions that then effected what the dream was - as if my interpretation steered the content (wch, of course, it did/does). Anyway, I wrote "KKK-like" because, while the people were wearing 'sheets' that covered their whole bodies & that had hoods on them w/ eye-holes, they weren't necessarily white sheets. They may've been silver. This may've segued abruptly into a scene w/ some people not disguised/ costumed by sheets w/ hoods, but in fairly ordinary clothes, carrying what appeared to be one gallon paint-buckets w/ black paint in them. Again, the 'interpreter/narrator' of the dream (my invisible self, my perspective) interpreted this as possible tar - making, apparently an effort to provide a narrative continuity between the last scene. The implication then became that the 1st group was KKK & the 2nd, much smaller group, was possibly going to tar someone. Instead, the buckets were filled w/ white paint (& I can remember myself/the observer trying to somehow explain the visible inside of the bucket walls being black by thinking that maybe the buckets had been used for black paint at one time & were now being reused for white). Sometime around here, I ceased to have only the 1st-person perspective, & became a character in the action - but, there still continued to be a detached observer viewpoint from wch I cd be perceived - so I became both perceiver & perceived. We (& it might've just turned into etta & myself here) started painting a medium-sized detached house w/ the white paint & various other objects near it - like lawn furniture? We weren't doing it as a 'job', this was a guerrilla action. Again, the 'observer' (myself) was observing the 'actors' (etta & myself - & possibly others who'd become unimportant to the observer) & imposing a narrative interpretation on what was happening. It's possible that 'because' the imposed narrative had become satisfactory to the observer that I then became an actor. The interpretation was that, perhaps, the 1st part of the dream w/ the KKK-like people was somehow historical, perhaps a film of a KKK event, & that this white painting was, perhaps, a modern day political action responding to this past. The meaning then became that we were, perhaps, performing a symbolic direct action by, perhaps, "white-washing" someone - the possibility being that we were "white-washing" the home of a politician or so-called investigator of something like the KKK who had white-washed over some political criminal behavior. I was very nervous performing this action - worried about the consequences - but still willing to take the risk because I thought it was important. The apparent man of the house, a somewhat overweight blustering moustached man in his 40s, came out & started aggressively interacting w/ us. At 1st there may've been a dog that may've been friendly & that dog may've turned more aggressively against us later. We stopped the painting, although we'd already done quite alot, & were negotiating w/ the man. Again, I was conscious of how the interpreter was changing the dream because I don't think that the man was carrying any weapons at 1st but then it was as if the interpreter decided that it was appropriate for his character for him to be carrying something so he was carrying something like a chain or w/ a chain as part of it. On the other hand, the interpreter wasn't always in control of steering the narrative either. This was demonstrated by near the end of the dream when a gangly girl, apparently the man's daughter, came up to & hugged my character telling me she "loved me". This was very confusing to my character because it made no sense in the interpreter's imposed logic of the scene - or, at least, it came from "left field". In other words, my character was thinking: Why? - as if expecting the girl to be more confused or hostile given that this apparent bit of direct symbolic action was directed against her apparent dad. The objects that we had painted on were gathered together in a pile & it

was as if we were being expected to haul them all away to restore them to their original condition.
Julie called to invite me out to lunch. Yeah!
Listened to 2 GREAT Pierre Henry pieces: "Une tour de Babel" & "Tokyo 2002".
Got emails from Ken Glanden & Zan Hoffman & Sterno - just like the good ole days!
Got a check loan for $500 from Dick Lahn for doing 3033 Brereton St Title Search.
Went out to eat w/ Julie & deposited check & food shopped.
Did some more research on 3033 Brereton.
Duped the Black Sheep Puppet Festival tapes for etta & myself.
Finally looked over my bank statements wch, as usual, I'd procrastinated on for mnths.
Witnessed afterEffects the documentary about the making of Effects & realized that my friend Barney McKenna was in it!!

Tuesday, December 6th, 2005EV

Worked a little on The Hardest Question Ever.
Rearranged my over-the-stairs hanging shirts.
Finally finished updated A Mere Outline.. & put it on-line.
Talked w/ Germ about the exciting last-minute details of her impending arrival!
Scanned Mont Royal Tim Ore painting.
Found a Priscilla McLean whale piece: "Beneath the Horizon III" for David Rothenberg.
Germ arrived at 4:35AMish at the train stn.
Hallelujah! SEX.

Wednesday, December 7th, 2005EV

Germ & I didn't get out of bed 'til about 4PM.
We met Julie & went to the Rock Room &
    Gooskie's & got free food from Julie's.

Thursday, December 8th, 2005EV

Germaine's still here & it's wonderful.
Watched preview of the Thai film Blissfully Yours.
Went to Church Brew Works.
Went to Potluck at Sean & Breen's &
    repossessed radio power supply.
Watched beginning of Henson's Labyrinth.
SEX.

Friday, December 9th, 2005EV

Germaine's still here & it's STILL wonderful.
Sold some records to Paul's CDs.
Found warehouse that Julie mentioned.
Had fun at Warhol event.
Finished watching Labyrinth.
SEX.

Saturday, December 10th, 2005EV

Went to AIR Gallery opening w/ Germ & Greg & Alisa & their 2 kids.
Checked out some of the Disinformation DVDs & other stuff w/ Germ.
SEX.

Sunday, December 11th, 2005EV

Finished reading Ibsen's <u>Ghosts</u>.
Germ is still visiting (& it's still great fun!).
Went to Jefferson Presents..
Watched the 3rd program of the Disinformation tv show.
SEX.

Monday, December 12th, 2005EV

SEX.
Got tooth #15 filled at the dental school by Lorraine.
Spent the day w/ Germ.
Have rc'vd 3 more boxes of my records in the mail from Owen.
Watched the 4th program of the Disinformation tv show.
Showed Germ the beginning of <u>Daisies</u>.

Tuesday, December 13th, 2005EV

Went w/ Germ to see the exhibit at the Wood St Gallery.
Sent off $500 √ for Title Search to law firm for 3033 Brereton.
Went w/ Germ to the Film Kitchen.
Went w/ Germ to Jacob & Elina & Kevin's place.
SEX.
Showed Germ the end of <u>Daisies</u>.

Wednesday, December 14th, 2005EV

Got $100 √ from Mom in mail today for X-Mas.
Worked on the <u>Haircut Paradox</u> movie.
Ross called to tell me about some work.

Thursday, December 15th, 2005EV

Germaine called me at 4:30AM to update me on her whereabouts & such-like.
Almost finished the <u>Haircut Paradox</u> movie.
Got a few emails from Germ telling me that her situation in Raleigh has calmed down a bit.
Andalusia invited me to her going away party.
Swifty invited me to his Hannukah party.
I fixed my bike tire again.
Jona called & we talked for a long time.

Friday, December 16th,

2005EV

Got a little work at the History Center.
Kalie left me a message inviting me to her place.
More or less finished the Haircut Paradox movie.
Talked briefly w/ Germ?

Saturday, December 17th, 2005EV

Made a birthday present for Mark & took it to his party.
Talked briefly w/ Germ.
Corrected the Haircut Paradox movie & made stills from it for the proposed Perverse Number Theory book.

Sunday, December 18th, 2005EV

Worked more on the Reactionary Muddle America scan retouches.

Monday, December 19th, 2005EV

Mailed off all my paid bills & presents for friends.
Grocery shopped.
Finished the Reactionary Muddle America scan retouches.
Typed the Bonnie Bonnell fashion interview into

the computer.
Met Mark, Julie, & her friend Ken at Gooski's.

Tuesday, December 20th, 2005EV

Finished typing the Bonnie Bonnell fashion interview into the computer.
Worked on the "Table of dIScONtENT" for footnotes.
Finished selecting the excerpts from & scanning in the relevant photos for Anonymous Family Reunion for footnotes.
Worked on the "Haircut Paradox" stills for the Perverse Number Theory book.
Talked w/ Jona on the phone about naming her production company.
Talked w/ Germ on the phone for an hr.

Wednesday, December 21st, 2005EV

Worked on my intro to footnotes.
Took Jesse McLean out to eat as a token appreciation for the help that she then gave in upgrading my computer in various ways - including installing Final Cut Pro, etc..
Also screened "Haircut Paradox" for Jesse. She liked it & asked questions.
etta asked me to go out to Duke's w/ her.
Installed the Skype program at Germ's suggestion & we proceeded to play w/

text-messaging. FUN!
Didn't drink alcohol.

Thursday, December 22nd, 2005EV

Finished the <u>footnotes</u> intro wch I think is very, very good.
Watched Bill Daniel's <u>Who is Bozo Texino?</u> wch had some pleasant surprises in it for me! Monty Cantsin & Buz Blurr being 2 of them.

Friday, December 23rd, 2005EV

Finished reading Queneau's <u>Odile</u> wch might be my favorite novel by him.
Finished writing the <u>Reactionary Muddle America</u> explanation for <u>footnotes</u>. I like it, I like it!
Talked w/ Germ via the Skype program for 'free' long distance thru the computer for the 1st time. Funzies!
Been listening to the Frederic Rzewski comp tapes that I assembled some time back. I'd forgotten that it's 5 volumes! Good stuff!
Went over to etta's for dinner w/ Grace & Katja & Alexi & Seth.
Didn't drink alcohol.

Saturday, December 24th,

2005EV

Looked at the inside of the Accu-Turn warehouse on the North Side.
Mark & Julie took me out to eat Indian food.
Wrote the entire "<u>t he book..</u> explanation".
Had a very long late-nite thru-the-Skype-program conversation w/ Germaine.

Sunday, December 25th, 2005EV

Photographed my "Spiral Tim(oo) Cal(oo)ndar" both filmically & digitally for <u>footnotes</u>.
Worked on loading the above into the computer & prepping them for the bk.
Talked w/ Germaine.
Went to Julie & Mark's for dinner & watched "Wondershowzen" episodes 105 thru 108.
etta came over & hung out.

Monday, December 26th, 2005EV

Made substantial progress on writing the "Dos & Don'ts of Dating" chapter of <u>footnotes</u>.
Didn't drink alcohol.

Tuesday, December 27th, 2005EV

Finished reading Che Elias' <u>Meddles Into Preclusion (Collected Poems</u>) book on SIX GALLERY PRESS.
Got the fotos I took Sunday developed.
Suzie called me & left a message.
Julie stopped by & gave me a mix tape.
FINISHED writing the 24pp "Dos & Don'ts of Dating" chapter of <u>footnotes</u>. Wch is something else.
Talked w/ Germ via Skype again! Yeah!

Wednesday, December 28th, 2005EV

Talked w/ Julie on the phone.
Figured out how to make PDF documents (VERY EASY!).
Went out to eat & drink w/ Kim. She decided she wants Joy & Babs' old apartment - wch helps them.
Talked w/ Suzie on the phone.
Printed out 2 copies of the 1st 39pp of <u>footnotes</u>.

Thursday, December 29th, 2005EV

Met Julie & did my laundry at her place & went to check on the condition of 3033 Brereton - wch was good.
Finished writing "l;a;n;g;u;a;g;e" for <u>footnotes</u> & printed it out.

Didn't drink alcohol.

Friday, December 30th, 2005EV

Finished the <u>Yet Another Slow-Burning Feast..</u>
    section for <u>footnotes</u> & got alot done on
    the <u>How to Write a Resumé</u> section.
Got a copy of the documentary on Bruce Haack
    & watched it.

Saturday, December 31st, 2005EV

Finished the <u>How to Write a Resumé</u> & <u>Telepathy
    Receptivity Training</u> sections for
    <u>footnotes</u> & printed them.
Made plans w/ Julie to go to Mikey's party &
    went to it & danced.

Sunday, January 1st, 2006EV

Got an answering machine message from Gen
    Ken that my <u>CircumSubstantial Playing &
    Blindfolded Tourism</u> CD is FINALLY
    finished (after almost 4&1/2 yrs!!)!!
Downloaded Bruce Haack's <u>Electric Lucifer</u> LP
    thanks to GERM.
Started working on & FINISHED a set of Terrence
    Dougherty samples & decided to
    combine playing them w/ a projection of

footage from the "Last Man on Earth"
    session that the samples are from.
Brainpang called & we talked.
An unknown person called & played a radio
    improv for the answering machine.
Jeanine called & we talked.
Worked some more on the "Mere Outline"
    section of footnotes.

Monday, January 2nd, 2006EV

Worked some more on the "Mere Outline"
    section of footnotes.
April called & we talked a bit.
I'm back in touch w/ Germ via Skype again!
    Hallelujah!!
Talked w/ Greg a bit about Peter Jackson's King
    Kong wch I haven't seen yet.
Finally got myself to work on "The Hardest
    Question Ever" in Final Cut Pro - despite
    my having almost no idea of how to use
    the program.
Talked w/ Julie on the phone & made plans to
    have lunch tomorrow.
Started working on the "Last Man on Earth" DVD
    for the UNCERT that I started working on
    the samples for yesterday.
Talked w/ Gen Ken on the phone & thanked him
    for the CD publishing.

Tuesday, January 3rd, 2006EV

Went out to eat w/ Julie.
etta came by & hung out.
Had a good conversation w/ Germ for a long time via Skype.
FINISHED THE 105 PAGE "Mere Outline" section for <u>footnotes</u>!!!!!
Finished watching all of the documentaries on the "special extended DVD edition" of Peter Jackson's <u>The Fellowship of the Ring</u>.
Didn't drink any alcohol.

<u>Wednesday, January 4th, 2006EV</u>

Worked on the "Reactionary Muddle America" section of <u>footnotes</u>.
Grocery shopped.
Watched the 1995 movie <u>The Corporation</u> about corporate mind control thru video games & sex CD-ROMs made in Las Vegas? funded by mafia? w/ lots of bodacious strippers?

<u>Thursday, January 5th, 2006EV</u>

Got the "Reactionary Muddle America" section up to 59pp.
The OUR-PUNK HOUSE people left some fruit & vegetable juices & a flower on my porch.
Kimberly called & wants me to meet a friend of

hers this wknd.
Didn't drink alcohol.

Friday, January 6th, 2006EV

Spent all day on the "Reactionary Muddle America" section.
Skype talked w/ Germ for 2 HOURS & she indulged my reading from "Reactionary.." obsession.
Didn't drink alcohol.

Saturday, January 7th, 2006EV

FINISHED the 101pp "Reactionary Muddle America" section of <u>footnotes</u>!
Finally watched Michael Moore's <u>Bowling for Columbine</u> wch was great!

Sunday, January 8th, 2006EV

Did the photo shoot for the "Wake Up Call" article today.
FINISHED reading Louis Aragon's <u>Paris Peasant</u> wch was great!
Went out to eat w/ Michael Pestel & a host of other friendly luminaries.
Printed out more of <u>footnotes</u>.
Didn't drink alcohol.

Monday, January 9th, 2006EV

Finished printing out "A Mere Outline.." & "AFR" parts of <u>footnotes</u>.
etta came by & we watched <u>Ghaath</u> - an Indian movie.

Tuesday, January 10th, 2006EV

etta bought me food to try to console me for the possible loss of my Warhol Museum job.
Worked on "Not Necessarily.." part of <u>footnotes</u>.
Finished reformatting "Death Bed Aerobics".
Didn't drink alcohol.

Wednesday, January 11th, 2006EV

An article about "Wake Up Call" w/ my picture in it came out in the Pittsburgh City Paper today.
Finished rereading Raymond Chandler's <u>The High Window</u>.
Didn't drink alcohol.

Thursday, January 12th, 2006EV

Worked more on <u>footnotes</u>.
Talked w/ Germ off & on for a few hrs.
Didn't drink alcohol.

<u>Friday, January 13th, 2006EV</u>

Drastically edited the "Movieography" I'd
    assembled for <u>footnotes</u> by cutting out
    all annotations.
Found another whale piece for David Rothenberg.
Didn't drink alcohol.

<u>Saturday, January 14th, 2006EV</u>

Finished reading Jonathan Lethem's <u>Amnesia
    Moon</u>.
Kevin Hicks gave me a ride home from work
    because I was sick.
Didn't drink alcohol.

<u>Sunday, January 15th, 2006EV</u>

etta gave me a ride to & from work because I'm
    still sick. Thanks to Kalie for loaning a
    vehicle.
Read all of Dashiell Hammett's <u>Woman in the
    Dark</u>.
Talked w/ Germaine.
etta brought by some banana bread that Kalie

made for me.
Almost finished the last part of <u>footnotes</u> - the "Movieography".
Didn't drink alcohol.

Monday, January 16th, 2006EV

FINISHED <u>footnotes</u> this morning.
Got an offer to have a short piece published by Public Guilt in Baltimore.
Finished the instrument titles for the <u>Last Man on Earth</u> movie & burned 2 DVDs of it.
Didn't drink alcohol.

Tuesday, January 17th, 2006EV

Sent off my resumé to Charlotte, NC where I might be able to get a good paying wk's work.
Didn't drink alcohol.

Wednesday, January 18th, 2006EV

Finished reading Patricia Highsmith's <u>The Two Faces of January</u>.
Kim called to ask me if I wanted to go to Swifty's Cabaret.
Talked w/ Julie.
Put all the <u>footnotes</u> files into one file & made it

a PDF.
Started working on the <u>Testes-3 Coming Out Party</u> transfer.
Didn't drink alcohol.

Thursday, January 19th, 2006EV

Wrote some text for the <u>Last Man on Earth</u> movie.
Made some scans for the <u>Testes-3 Coming Out Party</u> movie.
Talked briefly w/ Germ.
Didn't drink alcohol.

Friday, January 20th, 2006EV

Went thru the 1st 20pp of "Reactionary Muddle America" following Germ's crits.
Added new titles to <u>Last Man on Earth</u> w/ Jesse's on-phone help.
Finally watched <u>Guyana: Crime of the Century</u>. Grim, of course. But I'm glad I watched it.

Saturday, January 21st, 2006EV

Finally rc'vd the printer ink & the finished Generator CDs.
Talked w/ Germ before she left for Costa Rica.

Joined etta to watch a movie over at Kalie & Doug's where she was baby-sitting.

Sunday, January 22nd, 2006EV

Finished reading "James Tiptree, Jr"'s <u>The Starry Rift</u>.
Finished printing out 2 copies of <u>footnotes</u>.

Monday, January 23rd, 2006EV

Germ sent me an email from Costa Rica.
Sent off the <u>footnotes</u> ms to Che.
Went to the Dwelling House to talk about getting a mortgage.
Got more dental work done.
Bit the bullet & talked w/ lawyer Bill Ackerman & Joe Edelstein of Wiley Holdings about the Lis Pendens law-suit connected w/ 3033 Brereton.
Finally recorded 5 Terrence Dougherty Samples improvs.
Made an impromptu scratch edit using the "Last Man on Earth" Final Cut Pro file.
Watched "The Secret Life of Fax Machines".
etta came by & hung out.

Tuesday, January 24th, 2006EV

Applied for a job as an art handler at the CMoA.
Went to the library & checked out a slew of CDs.
Worked on adding graphics to the scratch edit
    ending of "Last Man on Earth".
Did my laundry & went out to the Rock Room w/
    Julie & Mark.

Wednesday, January 25th, 2006EV

Finished the footnotes cover.

Thursday, January 26th, 2006EV

Recorded some of the CDs I got from the library.
Didn't drink alcohol.

Friday, January 27th, 2006EV

Germaine's back from Costa Rica & we talked.
Didn't drink alcohol.

Saturday, January 28th, 2006EV

Finished reading Chuck Palahniuk's Invisible
    Monsters & read the entirety of Nick
    DiFinzo's the Worst Album Covers EVER!.
Went to a good Jefferson Presents... screening &

then the OUR-PUNK house-warming party.
Gen Ken told me that he(& Chop Shop?)'s sending me a $100 √ because he likes my work so much!!
Started systematically proofing <u>footnotes</u>.
Watched my 1st Frank Henenlotter film, <u>Brain Damage</u>.

Sunday, January 29th, 2006EV

Finished proofing the 1st 200pp of <u>footnotes</u>.
Talked w/ Germ via phone.
Watched "The Secret Life of the Photocopier".
Watched the 1st half of Warhol's <u>Blue Movie</u>.

Monday, January 30th, 2006EV

I took care of a slew of errands today: food shopping, mailing packages to Martin Heath & David Rothenberg, getting batteries & toothpaste & shoelaces, photocopying, returning CDs to the library, etc..
ALSO, got check for $100 from Generator wch will make it possible for me to financially 'survive' for the next 2 wks.
Proofed another 51pp of <u>footnotes</u>.
Finished watching Warhol's <u>Blue Movie</u> wch I think is a remarkable bit of "Cinema Verité".
Watched "The Secret Life of the Telephone".

Tuesday, January 31st, 2006EV

Finished the scratch edit ending of "Last Man on Earth".
Talked w/ Germ.
etta came over & we watched "The Secret Life of Quartz Watches".
Finished reading Patricia Highsmith's <u>Those Who Walk Away</u>.

Wednesday, February 1st, 2006EV

I didn't drink alcohol for 16 of the 31 days of January!
Julie photographed me today.
Proofread <u>footnotes</u> all the way up to page 406.
Watched the <u>Man With A Movie Camera</u> DVD w/ the Alloy Orchestra Soundtrack.
Checked out the <u>Fog Cycle</u> DVD again that those guys in Toronto gave me.
Burnt 3 copies of the full version of "Last Man on Earth" (w/ the complete scratch ending).

Thursday, February 2nd, 2006EV

Looked at 3450 Melwood today w/ Andrew the Impaled. It's not SPECTACULAR but it's

pretty good.
Started trying to arrange funding for 3450. Decided I prefer it to 3033 Brereton even though it's smaller. It's more practical & has a better yard & a nice 2nd floor enclosed porch & better location, etc.
Finished proofing <u>footnotes</u>.

Friday, February 3rd, 2006EV

Mailed off disc of corrected <u>footnotes</u> & the cover.
Thanks to mom I arranged to borrow $2,500 on my life insurance policy.
Didn't drink alcohol.

Saturday, February 4th, 2006EV

Got a great package of stuff from Germaine! Yum!
Kalie came thru for me & got me $500 to pay for the good faith cashier's check for the real estate company in connection w/ 3450 Melwood.
Went over all the paperwork w/ Andrew in prep for putting in my bid for 3450.
Talked w/ J9 on the phone. Her custody case seems optimistic.
Didn't drink alcohol.

Sunday, February 5th, 2006EV

No more working at the Warhol.
Finished the 1st Final Cut Pro 4 camera edit of
 "The Hardest Question Ever" &
 transferred it to mini-DV.
Watched Richard Elfman's Forbidden Zone - one
 of the DVDs Germ sent me.

Monday, February 6th, 2006EV

Didn't have to work today.
Found out that I may get $194 a WEEK from
 Unemployment!
Went to the Red, White & Blue Thrift store w/
 etta & friends & got some good clothes.
Talked w/ Ross Nugent about whether there was
 any projectionist work & about maybe
 having my book launching at Filmmakers.
Watched some of the Treasures from the
 SabuCat Archives DVD that Germ sent
 me. Good stuff!
Finished the "behind-the-scenes version" of "The
 Hardest Question Ever" & transferred it
 to mini-DV.

Tuesday, February 7th, 2006EV

Didn't have to work today.

Met Julie at the Rock Room for food & drink.

Wednesday, February 8th, 2006EV

Didn't have to work today.
Finished making the "The Hardest Question Ever" DVDs & mini-DVs.
Recorded 3 more improvs using the "Terrence Dougherty" samples taken from the "Last Man on Earth" session & burned a CD w/ the 1st 8 pieces.
Started amassing my iTunes Sampler Sampler COMPLETE (not really) "playlist" - it's quite alot more than I realized!! I've already collected 93 pieces & I'm not DONE YET!!
Didn't drink alcohol.

Thursday, February 9th, 2006EV

Didn't have to work today.
etta had lunch w/ me.
Recorded 3 more improvs using the "Terrence Dougherty" samples taken from the "Last Man on Earth" session & burned 2 CDs w/ the 1st 11 pieces.
Got alot done on my Sampler Sampler COMPLETE project.
Talked w/ Julie on the phone.
Recorded 2 "Gnome" samples improvs.
Watched William Greaves'

<u>Symbiopsychotaxiplasm Take 2 & 1/2</u>
wch was great.

Friday, February 10th, 2006EV

Didn't have to work today.
Repaid Kalie (& Zack) the $500 she (they)
    loaned me & hung out & talked w/ her
    for a while.
Hung out w/ Julie & she gave me a photo of
    myself & one of etta from the most
    recent photo session we did (wch I
    neglected to mention in this diary?).
Got the $2,500 loan & deposited it in a new
    money market account.
Recorded 8 more "Gnome" samples CDs &
burned all of them to disc.
Watched most of the "Sex & Drugs" DVD that
Germ sent me.
'Finished' assembling the "Sampler Sampler
(COMPLETE)".

Saturday, February 11th, 2006EV

Didn't have to work today.
Got a package w/ $30 & a vaudeo & 2 7"
    records etc from Chris of the Melted Men
    today.
etta gave me $20 that her mom sent her for
    Valentine's Day.
Germaine got back in contact.

Finished <u>Sampler Sampler 2</u> & burned 3 copies.
Went to the Big Idea benefit - quite a party (for Pittsburgh)!

Sunday, February 12th, 2006EV

Didn't have to work today.
Recorded 8 new versions of "Drum Machine" to add to the "Sampler Sampler (COMPLETE)".
Finished the REVISED <u>Sampler Sampler 2</u> (& I might revise it again!) & burned 3 copies.
Finished watching "Sex & Drugs".
Didn't drink alcohol.

Monday, February 13th, 2006EV

Didn't have to work today.
Put together packages for Free Speech TV, Che Elias, Michael Pestel, Chris of the Melted Men, & Locust Music & mailed them off.
Asked Anne-Marie at the History Center if there's any work there.
Called Geralyn & asked for names of people at the Science Center that might hire me.
Went to the library & checked out a bunch of Stefan Wolpe & Minoru Miki CDs & 2 movies & checked their job board.
Ross called & gave me work for Thursday & Friday.

Started recording a 4 volume <u>Stefan Wolpe
Revised Retrospective</u> - 6:17:19's worth
of material!
etta came by & we watch the beginning of <u>The
Two Towers</u>.

Tuesday, February 14th, 2006EV

Didn't have to work today.
Finished the <u>ASR-X MP3</u> 4 volume set (renamed
from "Sampler Sampler" to narrow the
focus) & burned the 1st of the CDs.
Finished up to volume 3 of the 4 volume <u>Stefan
Wolpe Revised Retrospective</u>.
Went to the Jerry Uelsmann exhibit at the
Manchester Craftsmen's Guild w/ Julie &
Mark.
Julie finished the English translation of Ajo's
"Micropoemas" for me.
Went to the Rock Room w/ Julie & Mark.
Buzzy Miller called me about my lack-of-work
situation.

Wednesday, February 15th, 2006EV

Didn't have to work today.
Joe Abeln called me to talk about my lack-of-
work situation.
Finished the last volume of the Wolpe
retrospective.
Burned to CD the last 3 volumes of the <u>ASR-X</u>

MP3 4 volume set.
Grocery shopped (the last day of my
    neighborhood supermarket.
etta came by.
Finished the 4 volume ASR-X MP3 MIX selections
    & burned them to CDs.
Julie repaid me $10.
Watched Once Upon A Time In China & liked it
    alot. It had an AMAZING fight scene w/
    ladders.
etta came by & we watched the end of Peter
    Jackson's The Two Towers.

Thursday, February 16th, 2006EV

Worked at the History Center & Ross told me I
    can get 2 steady days a wk for the next
    2 or 3 mnths.
Got the LIHEAP grant for $253 today for the gas
    bill.
etta came by & we watched all of Peter
    Jackson's Return of the King.

Friday, February 17th, 2006EV

Worked at the History Center.
Went to the Book 'Em benefit at the Brillo Box &
    shot some footage of the Baby Hollows
    & the Hollow Sisters.
Watched James Ivory's Savages.

Saturday, February 18th, 2006EV

Didn't have to work today.
Met Melissa Meinzer for lunch & was interviewed
 by her about "What's in a Name?" for a
 Pittsburgh City Paper article. Heather
 Mull'll probably photograph me for it.
etta came by.
Alisa called & invited me to her 40th birthday
 party tomorrow.
Went to Sean's place for his birthday party.

Sunday, February 19th, 2006EV

Didn't have to work today.
Filled out my 1st unemployment forms on-line.
Finished assembling the "ASR-X MP3 MIX
 SELECTION" & made liner notes for it &
 burned some copies.

Monday, February 20th, 2006EV

Got the repaired filmstrip camera back today
 PLUS Martin's "Car Wars" movie PLUS
 the B&W "Inauguration.." w/ the Partch
 soundtrack PLUS a lens adaptor for the
 filmstrip camera!!
Andrew the Impaled dropped off a list of housing
 inspectors for me & told me an idea

about a performance re health care that he's looking for a film & video-maker to assist w/.

Tuesday, February 21st, 2006EV

Didn't have to work today.
Arranged to meet a termite inspector on Thursday.
Partially paginated <u>footnotes</u> (as much as I'm going to).
Met Julie & Mark at the Rock Room.

Wednesday, February 22nd, 2006EV

Talked w/ Germ twice today. Gave her an ultimatum about deciding whether to come here or not.
Had dinner w/ the people interested in buying 3033 Brereton. They were nice & gave me food.
Started working on vaudeo for <u>footnotes</u> launching.
Didn't drink alcohol.

Thursday, February 23rd, 2006EV

Got offered a potentially good (temporary) job at the History Center organizing their

warehouse move.
Mailed off the final version of <u>footnotes</u>.
Hung out w/ etta.

<u>Friday, February 24th, 2006EV</u>

Got 5 new movies from Eide's.
Witnessed Harry Smith's <u>Mahagonny</u> at the
    Warhol.
Didn't drink alcohol.

<u>Saturday, February 25th, 2006EV</u>

Met John (of the shin guards) for the 1st time in
    at least a decade & Bobby & Valentina
    (from Sicily) who drove up from
    Baltimore to visit.
Got my 1st unemployment check!
Went to the Jefferson Presents annual Kuchar
    screening where I saw even more great
    George Kuchar films to add to my
    favorite films list.
Went to the Hollow Sisters show at the Waldorf
    school & wore my zipper clothes for
    Valentina's benefit. Unzipped one of the
    long arm zippers of the zipper jacket &
    Julie & I used it as a jump rope for
    people to dance w/. It was fun! [Is this
    beginning to read like a teenage girl's
    Barbie Diary?]
Went to Duke's & had good positive

conversations.
Julie told me that Valentina is strongly attracted to me - certainly something that's mutual & equally something that I don't feel I can pursue w/o causing much suffering for John. Sigh..

Sunday, February 26th, 2006EV

Went to Zenith w/ Mark & Julie & the B-More folks. Valentina professed her like-very-much (wch certainly came across as LOVE) for me. It was poetic & romantic in the strongest & best sense.
etta had dinner w/ me.
Watched Bulletproof Monk.
Didn't drink alcohol.

Monday, February 27th, 2006EV

Watched Raga Sagara. Not great but still interesting for me.
Talked w/ Julie about Valentina.

Tuesday, February 28th, 2006EV

Contacted Heather Toy about deinstalling the Bill Viola exhibit.
Read the "An Incomplete Map of Northern

Polarity" story that Germ sent me & wrote her about it.
Got hired for the Bill Viola deinstall.
Talked w/ Julie about Germaine & Valentina.
Talked w/ Jesse about Germaine & Valentina.
Finally read the libretto for those 3 1928 Wolpe pieces.
Talked w/ Germaine.
Didn't drink alcohol.

Wednesday, March 1st, 2006EV

Wrote an email to Valentina.
Talked w/ Julie about Germ & Valentina (mostly the latter) & wished her a good trip to Argentina.

Thursday, March 2nd, 2006EV

Worked (very briefly!) at the CMoA on the Viola deinstall.
Got $100 & passed it along to Julie to make available to Valentina for 'escape' money.
Had 3609 inspected for insect damage. It passed.
etta's back.
Ally came by & we chatted.
Scanned more stuff for the hypothetical revised "Poop & Pee Dog.." (etc) movie.
Finished reading Flann O'Brien's <u>The Hair of the</u>

<u>Dogma</u>.
Watched <u>Scary Movie 3</u>.

Friday, March 3rd, 2006EV

Didn't have to work today.
Talked w/ Valentina for 3 hrs!
etta came by & spent the nite.

Saturday, March 4th, 2006EV

Didn't have to work today.
Finished watching G. W. Pabst's version of <u>The Threepenny Opera</u>.
Finished the scans for the revised <u>Poop & Pee Dog Copyright Violation Ceremony</u> movie & entered some relevant footage into the computer.
Did the paperwork for bidding on another house.
Watched all of Bernd Alois Zimmermann's over-the-top opera <u>Die Soldaten</u>.

Sunday, March 5th, 2006EV

Talked w/ Germ for about 3 hrs.
Talked w/ J9 for an hr.
Didn't drink alcohol.

Monday, March 6th, 2006EV

Talked w/ Valentina for an hr & a half.
Asked Gretchen to go to Washington DC w/ me

& she sd yes.
Talked w/ Dave Scheper about the raid on his house.
Watched a British TV production of Stravinsky's Oedipus Rex.
etta came by & spent the nite.

Tuesday, March 7th, 2006EV

Sent off yet another 'final' version of footnotes today.
Settled on $17,000 for 3609 Melwood today.
Watched a somewhat experimental video production of Stravinsky's The Flood.
Got 2 emails from Julie from Argentina.

Wednesday, March 8th, 2006EV

The "Game of the Name" PGH CP article came out today w/ the interview w/ me in it.
Talked w/ Valentina.
Went grocery shopping w/ etta tonight. Kalie & Doug loaned their car & etta got me food.
etta came by & I showed her Hellzapoppin'.
Didn't drink alcohol.

Thursday, March 9th, 2006EV

Got the contract for "Diszey Spots"'s airing on Free Speech TV today.
Watched Tarkovky's 1st student film, "The Killers", wch was psychologically extraordinarily compelling for something done by people so young (of course it's origin in Hemingway helped!).
Had a talk w/ Germaine.
Didn't drink alcohol.

Friday, March 10th, 2006EV

Managed to get a fairly good nite's sleep.
Worked on the revised version of "T he Poop & Pee Dog Copyright Violation Ceremony" movie.
Got an invite to a wine & cheese party at the History Center.
Got a VERY sweet email from Valentina.
Got some positive emails from Germaine.
Talked w/ Brainpang.
etta came by & we watched a movie.
Didn't drink alcohol.

Saturday, March 11th, 2006EV

Hung out at etta's w/ the "boat kids" & Erok & such-like folks..

Sunday, March 12th, 2006EV

Watched/Listened-to quasi-documentary about
    Ives called <u>Charles Ives: A Good
    Dissonance Like A Man</u>
    - wch made me love Ives' music all the
more!

Monday, March 13th, 2006EV

Talked w/ Valentina.
Andrew the Impaled came by to drop off the
    house contract.
etta came by & we watched <u>Magical Mystery
    Tour</u>,

Tuesday, March 14th, 2006EV

'Finished' the <u>B.T.O.U.C.</u> movie.

Wednesday, March 15th, 2006EV

Added a few more 'finishing' touches to the
    <u>B.T.O.U.C.</u> movie & dumped the <u>booed
    usic</u> movie into the computer so I cd
    then start burning an <u>'80s Night</u> DVD w/
    the 2 of them on it.
Watched a movie of the Parisian 1995
    production of Janacek's <u>The Cunning
    Little Vixen</u>.

Thursday, March 16th, 2006EV

Got check for $5,000 from dad.
Sent off signed mortgage papers.
Worked on trying to burn DVDs of "'80s Night".

Friday, March 17th, 2006EV

Arranged for homeowner's insurance.
Witnessed movie versions of 2 short operas:
> Leonard Bernstein's "Trouble in Tahiti" &
> Bela Bartok's "Bluebeard's Castle" - both
> fairly interesting.

Went to Sean & Breen's for a party & had fun.

Saturday, March 18th, 2006EV

Suzie called.
Participated in the anti-war march
> commemorating the 3rd yr of the war
> against Iraq.

Germaine called TWICE.
Jona emailed after having returned from Bulgaria
> & sd she's thinking of buying property in
> Pittsburgh.

Managed to finally output "B.T.O.U.C." to DVD
> thanks to Toast Titanium.

etta came by.

Sunday, March 19th,

2006EV

Germaine called again! YEAH!
Started the outputting of the 6 "footnotes
   movies" to DVD.
Didn't drink alcohol.

Monday, March 20th, 2006EV

Talked w/ Valentina. She's coming to Pittsburgh
   tomorrow w/ Julie!
etta came by & we watched some Grant Munro
   movies.

Tuesday, March 21st, 2006EV

I succeeded in finally outputting "B.T.O.U.C." to
   mini-dv.
Mailed off alotof packages - including the stuff to
   Bill O'Driscoll relevant to my book
   launching.
Julie & Valentina came over & we went out to
   drink & eat. Then etta came by & I
   screened "B.T.O.U.C." for all of them.

Wednesday, March 22nd, 2006EV

Hung out w/ Valentina - "she wanna make sex

with me so bad & she dreamin' about ooooooooooooooooooooooooooooomiiiiii iiiiiiiiiiigod!" Then she sd "I'm gonna do it tonight if somebody don't kill me 1st" BUT, we're not really do anything. Hung out w/ Julie too who's feeling better.
Uploaded "Official..Institutions" movie.

Thursday, March 23rd, 2006EV

Julie & Mark got back together.
Valentina & I went to the Mattress Factory & made out all day.
Had dinner w/ V & M & J & etta.

Friday, March 24th, 2006EV

Valentina stayed an extra day. More intensity between us.
Julie photographed her at the Allegheny Cemetery.
'Watched' 2 vampire movies together.
Went out to Duke's. More passionate hugging, kissing, touching.

Saturday, March 25th, 2006EV

Finished marking chapters & burning DVDs of "Official..Institutions" movie.
Attended Jefferson Presents screening.

Sunday, March 26th, 2006EV

Exchanged emails w/ Valentina & arranged for
    her to talk w/ Angela Guarda tomorrow
    in case she needs mental health / legal
    advice.
Made substantial progress on the Final Cut Pro
    remake of "Haircut Paradox".

Monday, March 27th, 2006EV

Got 2 publications from Bruce Stater in the mail
    today.
Julie came by & we talked.
Talked w/ Valentina on the phone.
Arranged for Brian Dean Richmond to look at the
    sink situation at the new house
    tomorrow.
Finished watching <u>Lulu</u>.

Tuesday, March 28th, 2006EV

BDR looked at the plumbing situation in the new
    house & we went out & bought some
    supplies.
Talked w/ Valentina on the phone.
Met Julie for food & drinks.

Wednesday, March 29th, 2006EV

Finally wrote to Germ saying our relationship is ended. [This is only "positive" in the sense that it involves an attempt at closure]
Talked w/ Valentina.
Went to a Freedom of Information Act Request meeting at the Thomas Merton Center.
Visited Julie & Filmmakers & saw her recent prints.
Watched George Romero's <u>Land of the Dead</u> & the relevant extras.

Thursday, March 30th, 2006EV

Got gas turned on at 3609.
Showed Julie 3609 & she liked it.
Had lunch w/ Julie.
Went to library.
Showed etta 3609 & she liked it.
Suzie & Matt & Jasmine are back!!
Didn't drink alcohol.

Friday, March 31st, 2006EV

Hung out w/ Suzie & Matt & Jasmine & Julie.
Went to hear Jesse & Thad play at the Wood St Gallery.
Matt Gleeson & friends arrived to spend the night before driving on to Indianapolis.

Saturday, April 1st, 2006EV

Chris Deane & Brian Dean Richmond started on
	the plumbing of 3609.
Met the neighbors of 3609 a little.
Joy & Matt & another guy saw my house.
Julie came by & called Valentina to check on her.
Watched Takashi Shimizu's [2nd version of?] <u>The
	Grudge</u>.
Didn't drink alcohol.

Sunday, April 2nd, 2006EV

Talked w/ Germaine for what seems like the 1st
	time in a long time. [Once again, the
	ambiguity of what's positive or not
	positive is extreme here! It's positive
	that I'm still capable of an open dialog
	w/ someone whose relationship has been
	so deeply connected to my despair but
	it's not positive that talking w/ Germaine
	can lure me away from the clear thinking
	I so desperately 'need' in relation to
	Valentina.]
'Performed' my "Last Man on Earth" piece at
	Modern Formations on the same bill w/
	Kevin Hicks & friends & the Australians:
	Dimitra; & The Stabs.

Monday, April 3rd, 2006EV

etta's back from FL. She & the Aussies & I hung
	out. I showed Matt 2 hrs of "Don't Walk

Backwards".
Talked w/ Valentina for almost 2 hrs.

Tuesday, April 4th, 2006EV

Told Germaine that it's alright for her to come here to visit this wknd.
Closed on 3609 Melwood.
Talked w/ Valentina. SHE might come visit next wk..
Visited Suzie & Matt & Jasmine's place. Matt showed me his Waldorf synthesizer.
Talked w/ neighbor Dave at the Rock Room.

Wednesday, April 5th, 2006EV

Didn't drink alcohol.

Thursday, April 6th, 2006EV

Talked w/ Germ.
Talked w/ Valentina.
Took Suzie out to eat at Dave's for her birthday (+ Matt & Jasmine & Julie).
Took etta out to get food from Dave's.
Watched Charles Atlas' <u>The Legend of Leigh Bowery</u> w/ etta.

Friday, April 7th, 2006EV

Brian & Chris (probably) FINALLY finished the plumbing.

Attended the 1st of the Robert Haller nights at
>   Filmmakers.
Went to Doug's birthday party.

Saturday, April 8th, 2006EV

Tore up some of the linoleum at 3609.
Finished the version of "Last Man on Earth" w/
>   the Modern Formations soundtrack.
Went to the 2nd Haller night.

Sunday, April 9th, 2006EV

Valentina called me to console me about
>   Germaine.
Started working on "Radical History Bike Tour"
>   movie.
Screened "Subtitles (16mm version)" for Robert
>   Haller at Filmmakers - & watched films
>   by other locals.

Monday, April 10th, 2006EV

Talked w/ Valentina.
Didn't drink alcohol.

Tuesday, April 11th, 2006EV

Had water turned on at 3609.
Talked w/ Valentina.
Attended Film Kitchen.
Went out w/ Julie for a drink.
Finished the long version of "Radical History Bike

Tour" [no longer extant as of a few days later].

Wednesday, April 12th, 2006EV

Chris Deane & Brian Richmond worked on the 3609 plumbing some more.
Tore up more linoleum at 3609.
Emailed out the invite to the proposed 3809 NUDIST MASK PARTY.
Worked on the short version of "Radical History Bike Tour" & found mistakes in the long one.
Got a case of beer & hung out w/ Julie at 3609.
Hung out w/ etta.

Thursday, April 13th, 2006EV

Fantastic spring weather is here!
Grocery shopped some Indian food.
Ally came by & we talked about sound, etc..
Julie came by & we talked & went to her place for awhile.
Didn't drink alcohol.

Friday, April 14th, 2006EV

Finally managed to produce an [almost] passable DVD of "Pittsburgh Radical History Tour".
Julie stopped by.

Watched [the deliberately misleadingly named
　　　Jackie Chan's] Bloodpact wch seemed
　　　like a precursor to Drunken Master & was
　　　pretty funny.

Saturday, April 15th, 2006EV

Started sanding the floors at 3609.

Sunday, April 16th, 2006EV

Went to Schenley Park for Julie's 31st birthday
　　　picnic & hung out w/ Julie, Mark, Suzie,
　　　Matt, Jill, Jasmine, & Ben. It was fun to
　　　be forced out of my routines by Jasmine
　　　- to play tag & such-like things.

Monday, April 17th, 2006EV

FINALLY managed to burn an acceptable DVD of
　　　"Pittsburgh Radical History Tour" & to
　　　transfer it to mini-DV.
Got film & vaudeo to shoot for NUDIST MASK
　　　PARTY.
Talked w/ Julie at Filmmakers.
Had dinner w/ etta.

Tuesday, April 18th, 2006EV

Mailed off a bunch of packages & paid some bills.
Did my laundry.
Visited Julie at Filmmakers.

Talked w/ Bernard on the phone.
Watched Eric Fleischauer's DVD.
etta came by & watched a bit of <u>Winged Migration</u>.

Wednesday, April 19th, 2006EV

Borrowed Doug & Kalie's car to get stuff for the new house & to get groceries & send off mail, etc..
Started making the big run of "The Hardest Question Ever" DVDs.
Finished reading the 1st issue of "Ecriture".
Compiled 6 of my laptop-edited movies onto a 160 minute VHS tape.
Recorded Julie's birthday phone messages for her.
Put in a token supporting appearance at the Indicator Species tour benefit.
Finished watching <u>Tetsuo: The Iron Man</u> on video.

Thursday, April 20th, 2006EV

Ally came by & returned the stuff she'd borrowed.
etta & I ran errands in Mary's car - including her getting more groceries for me from the Co-Op.
Didn't drink alcohol.

Friday, April 21st, 2006EV

Finished making 50 of the "The Hardest Question Ever" DVDs.

Got pd $206 by Citizen Cinema for "Diszey Spots".

Finished reading vol 1 # 6 of Golden Handcuffs Review (wch has a poem by Bruce Stater in it).

Worked on "Imagine Utopias" movie.

Didn't drink alcohol.

Saturday, April 22nd, 2006EV

Finished "Imagine Utopias" movie.

Rc'vd Unemployment Compensation for $95.

Edited Julie's Birthday Messages tape for her.

Spat & etta showed up at 6:40 for the NUDIST MASK PARTY! The final tally of attendees to this was the aforementioned + Erok + James & Laura + Julie + Margaret + Marcus + Ben Shannon + Matt (recently arrived to the Boat Kids).

Sunday, April 23rd, 2006EV

Ate dinner at Mark & Julie's Vegan Mexican potluck.

Didn't drink alcohol.

Monday, April 24th, 2006EV

Watched & copied the "Tool Dissectional"
vaudeo loaned to me by Craig B - wch, if
not outright made by The Brothers Quay
was heavily influenced by them.
Copied "The Brothers Quay Collection" for Craig
& pulled out 2 copies of
DDC#040,002#3 for him because he
mentioned an interest in Alex Grey.
Didn't drink alcohol.

Tuesday, April 25th, 2006EV

Checked the plumbing at 3609 - wch BDR seems
to've finally finished satisfactorily.
Had a pleasant conversation w/ Valentina.
Dumped Vermin's "Fake Reporter" footage into
the computer for IMP ACTIVISM 7.
Worked on other parts of IMP ACTIVISM 7.
Didn't drink alcohol.

Wednesday, April 26th, 2006EV

Attended Matt & Suzie's "Weird Haircut Party"
where I gave them 3 of my haircut
photocopies & read "Haircut Paradox" &
wore my Hir Suit & that thick stiff rubber
hairpiece.
Worked on IMP ACTIVISM 7.
Didn't drink alcohol.

Thursday, April 27th, 2006EV

Was given "Powers of Ten Interactive" disc
(based on the movie by Charles & Ray
Eames) by Betty Hase of Herman Miller,
Inc - she gave a presentation at the
Warhol Museum that I worked for.
Finished "Steelers Fans Against War" - my 255th
movie!
Didn't drink alcohol.

Friday, April 28th, 2006EV

Dumped the Brillo Box Book 'Em Benefit footage
into the computer.
Had a long talk w/ Jeanine.
Talked w/ Julie.
Watched Peter Brooks' <u>Meeting with Remarkable Men</u> about Gurdjieff's early years.

Saturday, April 29th, 2006EV

Made a good bit of moolah working 2 jobs today.
etta came by & spent the night.
Didn't drink alcohol.

Sunday, April 30th, 2006EV

Attended Film Kitchenette at the Shadow Lounge
where I got to see excerpts from all the
Film Kitchen TVs.
Suzie & Jasmine came by & hung out & then Dan
& his dog Cosmos dropped by too.

The Lahns contributed the $500 they loaned me to my new house.
Went out to eat at the Church Brew Works w/ etta & her parents.
etta came by & we watched the beginning of Merchant Ivory's <u>Mystic Masseur</u>.
Drank - but the total days w/o alcohol this mnth was 12. Not bad.

Monday, May 1st, 2006EV

Gave etta a copy of "Steelers Fans Against War" for her 32nd birthday.
Finished editing a raw version of the "Book 'Em Benefit" to be used in "Book 'Em".
Talked w/ Julie.
Finished watching <u>Mystic Masseur</u>.

Tuesday, May 2nd, 2006EV

Finished reading Joan Slonczewski's <u>The Children Star</u>.
Didn't drink alcohol.

Wednesday, May 3rd, 2006EV

Went out for a drink w/ Ross, Sam, & Patrick after work.
Went to Julie & Mark's for dinner w/ Suzie & Matt & Jasmine & others.
Met Marissa & Kalie on the way home & showed them 3609.

Thursday, May 4th, 2006EV

[I shd perhaps note here that these days for wch
 the entries are minimal are usually days
 when I'm working alot. Eg, Tuesday &
 today I worked 2 jobs - as I will
 tomorrow. I don't usually consider work
 to be a positive thing because I largely
 feel forced into it by capitalism (simple
 version). HOWEVER, I can fairly say that
 the up-side of work is that I've learned
 various useful skills thru it that I might
 not have otherwise. These days I've
 been learning alot about crate building
 for artifacts & have had some fun
 making custom armatures for shipping
 life-size figure sculptures that're part of
 the "Clash of Empires" exhibit. That's
 been largely positive.]
Didn't drink alcohol.

Friday, May 5th, 2006EV

Pete, from the Education Dept of the AWM &
 from the band Air Guitar Magazine,
 asked me if I wanted to play in an
 improvisor's event at the Brillo Box in
 July.
Didn't drink alcohol.

Saturday, May 6th, 2006EV

Worked on the "Book 'Em at the Post Office"

section of the "Book 'Em" quasi-
documentary.
Repaired my guitar case somewhat.
Practiced playing guitar w/ the Ebow.
Talked w/ Julie on the phone.
etta came by & we hung out & talked & she
spent the night.

Sunday, May 7th, 2006EV

Practiced playing guitar some more.
Worked on the "Book 'Em at the Post Office"
section some more.
Gordon Nelson invited me over to his & Tara's
place to watch films.
Met Joy & LaFawn on Liberty Ave & talked w/
them for a bit.

Monday, May 8th, 2006EV

Valentina called me.
Worked on "Book 'Em at the Post Office" more.
Ally called me to talk about Genet's <u>Our Lady of
the Flowers</u> etc.
Witnessed John Cassavetes' <u>The Killing of a
Chinese Bookie</u>.
etta came by & spent the night.

Tuesday, May 9th, 2006EV

Julie loaned me her van & I used it to transport a
vacuum cleaner & a rug I bought & to
move 6 of my 8 file cabinets & a few
other odds & ends to 3609. Julie helped

w/ much of that.
Mailed off <u>Story of a Fructiferous Society</u> to the Lausanne Film & Music festival & another copy of the same (in VHS) to Anthology.
Finished editing down the "Book 'Em at the Post Office" footage to 14:41.
Finally got the last of the floor detritus trash out of 3609.
Didn't drink alcohol.

Wednesday, May 10th, 2006EV

Arranged the file cabinets at 3609 & wood-puttied & polyurethaned some of the floors.
Started working on a maze movie called "abhilnrty".
Jesse McLean gave me tech assistance.
Checked out <u>The Believer</u> - a great movie about Jews/Neo-Nazis.

Thursday, May 11th, 2006EV

Worked more on "abhilnrty" - rotating the image - thusly taking advantage of FCP features that I wasn't previously familiar w/.
Met Julie at a photography opening at Filmmakers & then we went to the Rickety House to hang out w/ some of my favorite Filmmakers folks: Tony,

Adam, Eric, & Jesse.

Friday, May 12th, 2006EV

Installed 2 new locks at 3609 & moved 2 more loads of stuff there.
Worked more on "abhilnrty".
Talked w/ Jarrett at the Warhol.
Didn't drink alcohol.

Saturday, May 13th, 2006EV

Moved more stuff into 3609.
Worked more on "abhilnrty".
Didn't drink alcohol.

Sunday, May 14th, 2006EV

Checked out Shaun's Tin-Can Telephone stretching across the Hollow.
Alexi helped me move some records & CDs to 3609.
Hung out w/ Alexi & Andalusia & Marcus & etta & some of the Boat Kids at etta's & took them to see 3609.
Worked more on "abhilnrty".
Watched Werner Herzog's <u>The Invincible</u> w/ etta.

Monday, May 15th, 2006EV

Got a fairly hefty paycheck from the History Center - enabling me to pay the overdue 3809 gas bill.

Moved more (m)usic equipment to 3609.
Worked more on "abhilnrty".
Grocery shopped.
etta came by & hung out & spent the night.
Didn't drink alcohol.

Tuesday, May 16th, 2006EV

Found out where the Birmingham Free Medical
   Clinic is so I can get my kidneys (etc)
   checked out.
Finally got the checks I ordered 4 wks ago & got
   paying most of the bills out of the way.
Worked more on "abhilnrty".
Moved more (m)usic equipment to 3609.
Went to Paul's Lumber & Bloomfield Hardware &
   got supplies for 3609.
Started building shelves at 3609.
Finished watching Pabst's <u>Pandora's Box</u>.
FINALLY finished reading Kane X, Faucher's
   <u>URDOXA</u>, the 2nd bk I've read published
   by Six Gallery Press & something I've
   been plowing thru for at least 4 mnths
   (?).
Didn't drink alcohol.

Wednesday, May 17th, 2006EV

Started reading <u>The Professor and the Madman</u>
   (that Craig had given me).
Made $75 (minus taxes) for an incredibly easy
   job at the Warhol.
Picked up 2 cheap CDs: Yuji Takahashi's <u>Finger</u>

Light & Philip Johnston & the Transparent Quartet's The Merry Frolics of Satan (The Georges Méliès Project).
Went to the Birmingham Health Clinic & got an exam that provisionally announced me as being in good health - probably w/o hepatitis or kidney problems.
Hung out w/ etta briefly.
Hung out w/ Julie briefly.
Finished editing "abhilnrty" - my 256th movie!
Didn't drink alcohol.

Thursday, May 18th, 2006EV

Moved another vanload to 3609.
Installed 5 utility shelves along 1 wall of the future library of 3609.
Wrote the "diSTILLed Life Afterwords".
Hung out w/ etta & Alexi & Mary Mac a little.
Witnessed the overture (or prelude?) & 1st act of Syberberg's version of Wagner's Parsifal.

Friday, May 19th, 2006EV

Got a radio transmitter gas meter installed at 3609 so I can get accurate gas bills instead of overestimates.
Got more supplies for 3609 & worked on reinforcing the shelves.
Finished listening to all the tapes I have filed under "miscellaneous" in the order in wch they're organized - I don't

remember when I started this but it probably took mnths. It's quite a collection. The comp from Greg Pierce is probably the 'winner' for diversity!
Made $150+ (minus taxes) for 2 incredibly easy 'consulting' jobs at the Warhol.
Got the <u>Experimental Cinema of the 1920s and 1930s</u> double DVD set.
Went to the birthday party for Dore & Lucha.
Watched the 4 Man Ray films & "The Life & Death of 9413 A Hollywood Extra" of the above DVD set.
Didn't drink alcohol.

Saturday, May 20th, 2006EV

Moved a vanload of books to 3609.
Went to Schenley Park w/ Julie & her friends Jessica & Jeff from Baltimore.
Worked on the bookshelves at 3609 some more.
Went to the TBA Records release party at the Quiet Storm for the Pimps Up Hoedown / Hollow Sisters 7".
Watched "Ménilmontant" from the <u>Experimental Cinema</u> DVDs.

Sunday, May 21st, 2006EV

Finished the "NuVie House" intro to the "Book 'Em" documentary.
Watched "Brumes D'Automne" & "Lot In Sodom". Loved the latter. Also watched Hans Richter's "Rhythmus 21" & "Vormittagsspuk" (Ghosts Before Breakfast) - enjoyed the latter once

again.
Didn't drink alcohol.

Monday, May 22nd, 2006EV

Started putting books on the shelves at 3609.
    Moved more books & tapes there, etc..
Worked on the Book 'Em documentary more.
Hung out w/ etta & talked about Little Antoine - her friend who just got out of prison today.
Witnessed the rest of the <u>Experimental Cinema</u> DVD #1 & the 1st 2 of #2.

Tuesday, May 23rd, 2006EV

Barb Antel called offering to help me move.
Have the 3609 library installed up to "Film" now
    & set up the file cabinets in the middle of the room around the portable book cases I made many yrs ago. Put some of the SF bks in those.
Hung out w/ Julie at Filmmakers & got free pizza.
Made dinner for etta, who spent the night, & finished watching the <u>Experimental Cinema</u> DVD #2.

Wednesday, May 24th, 2006EV

Didn't have to work.
Spent most of the day working on the 3609 library more. Have 4 more shelves built

& I started putting the Literature section on them.
Matt came by & hung out a little while I was doing the above.
Worked on organizing the <u>Book 'Em</u> material in FCP.
Started reading <u>Whalesong</u>.

Thursday, May 25th, 2006EV

Awoke from a wonderful prolonged flying dream where I was flying both inside & outside on a college campus. Inside I was bouncing back & forth between walls & a girl student invited me to do something w/ her saying something like "I've never tried that rock climbing technique before" in reference to my flying.
Saw an ad for <u>footnotes</u> on-line - thanks to Booksurge.
Worked more on organizing the <u>Book 'Em</u> footage.
Moved another vanload of books to 3609.
Finished reading <u>The Professor and the Madman</u>.
Hung out at etta's & chatted for a while.
Didn't drink alcohol.

Friday, May 26th, 2006EV

Spent the majority of the day moving my library from 3809 to 3609. Got the 3609 library installed up to & thru all of Literature - 2 walls covered w/ books!

Remet Mark, my 3611 neighbor, &
Catherine (the nice real estate agent).
Finished witnessing Syberberg's version of
Wagner's <u>Parsifal</u>.

<u>Saturday, May 27th, 2006EV</u>

Worked on the 3609 library some more.
Didn't drink alcohol.

<u>Sunday, May 28th, 2006EV</u>

Moved the last vanload of books.
Went to Jill's 28th birthday party.

<u>Monday, May 29th, 2006EV</u>

Hung out w/ Julie a little.
etta came by & we talked for over an hr & she
spent the nite.

<u>Tuesday, May 30th, 2006EV</u>

Made a very simple PhotoShop 'collage' of
Michael Pestel & the newborn Josey &
emailed it to him & Elise.
Grocery shopped.
Worked on <u>Book 'Em</u> more - edited about the 1st
6:40.
Finished checking out the <u>Treasures from the
SabuCat Archives</u> DVD that Germaine
sent me a while back.
Checked out the 1st 3 Sid Laverents films on the

DVD Germ sent me! Great stuff! He's the George Kuchar of (slightly more) normal life! Will probably add these to my favorite films list.

Wednesday, May 31st, 2006EV

Moved another vanload to 3609 & worked on the library more.
Talked to Tony Balko & Evan & Ben of the Boat Kids in Bloomfield.
Talked w/ Shaun & Ally by Mikey's place.
Bought 8 records from Mikey for generously cheap prices ($23 total!).
Joined Mikey & Julie & Debs at Duke's for its hypothetical final nite.
Drank - but didn't drink 13 days this mnth - better than the 12 of last mnth.

Thursday, June 1st, 2006EV

Installed the final bookshelves for the 3609 library. I shd be able to have that rm finished in another day or so.
Worked on "Book 'Em" some more.
Made plans to see movies w/ Julie tomorrow nite.
Hung out w/ etta & she gave me a packaged copy of "The Hardest Question Ever" DVD.
Didn't drink alcohol.

Friday, June 2nd, 2006EV

Got some more supplies (mostly wood) for 3609.
Worked ever so slightly on "Book 'Em".
Went out w/ Julie to an opening connected to the 3 Rivers Arts Festival.

Saturday, June 3rd, 2006EV

FINALLY GOT THE PROOF OF footnotes & IT LOOKS GREAT (except for a few minor mistakes).
Got 12 more records from Mikey S for very cheap.
Corrected the proof of footnotes.
Went to the benefit party for Erin & Scott.
Watched the last of the Sid Laverents movies - about his dog "Heidi".

Sunday, June 4th, 2006EV

Started on the record shelves in the (M)Usic rm at 3609.
Worked on the "Book 'Em" movie.
Added Sid Laverents films to my favorites list online.
Witnessed Outfoxed & the DVD extras.

Monday, June 5th, 2006EV

Took care of various bills & debts.
Sent off a new disc of footnotes to Che &

immediately thereafter discovered yet another typo!
Replaced both my bike tires finally.
Discovered TWO MORE MISTAKES in <u>footnotes</u> - 1 of them major. Decided to send another disc to Che tomorrow.
Didn't drink alcohol.

Tuesday, June 6th, 2006EV

Ran 'early' morning errands - including some minimal grocery shopping.
Talked a little w/ Tracey Mortimer about doing some jobs on 3809 & 3609.
Talked w/ Doug Retzler.
Corrected <u>footnotes</u> YET AGAIN & mailed the disc off to Che.
Finished the record shelves & made the CD shelves at 3609.
Worked on "Book 'Em" doc more.
Didn't drink alcohol.

Wednesday, June 7th, 2006EV

Finished putting the CDs on shelves at 3609 & set up most of the Erector Set.
Didn't drink alcohol.

Thursday, June 8th, 2006EV

Got emails from Doug about his Autoternative show.

CRUST CAME BY! 1st time I've seen him since he went to jail for stealing beer!
Started making copies of IMP ACTIVISMs 2,4, & 5 for Doug.
Showed my proof of <u>footnotes</u> to neighbor Mark.
The Indicator Species rehearsal at the Warhol went ok.
Watched Steve James' movie <u>Stevie</u>. Quite a dose. To put it mildly.

Friday, June 9th, 2006EV

Reassembled the glass marimba at 3609.
The Indicator Species performance at the Warhol was well-attended & well-appreciated.
Finally went to the Belvedere's bar where Joy bartends & hung out w/ friends there.

Saturday, June 10th, 2006EV

Geof Huth emailed me!
All in all.. a strangely positive day..
Made substantial progress on the (M)Usic Rm at 3609.
Talked w/ the neighbor about whether pr not I'd sideswiped his car on Sunday, May 28th, & he was a decent fellow. [This is yet another instance where the constraints of this POSITIVE diary make such an entry stand out because of its lack of context - the original incident having been quite distressing.]
Worked a very stressful wedding at the Warhol

where 2 guys who seemed to be somewhat familiar w/ my 'work' where very respectful & friendly. Also talked w/ a reasonably well-informed fairly new GA there named Eric about subjects of some interest to me.

Finished reading Robert Siegel's Whalesong & started reading Vonnegut's Hocus Pocus.

THEN, on the way home I very coincidentally crossed paths w/ Julie outside the Rock Room so I joined her & Mark & his dad & others for a couple of drinks.

Sunday, June 11th, 2006EV

Moved a vanload of all the Widémouth stuff to 3609 & made substantial progress there on setting up the (M)Usic room.

Hung out w/ Julie for a while & she played me her friend Ben's song inspired by hearing about me from "Leg Armor" John: "3D Brain of Mr. Brain" by Space Monsters (an English noise band from around the early '80s).

Alan Lord sent me an MP3 of a song he plays on from 1979.

Witnessed the heavy-handed (but still very interesting) Shipbreaking documentary that Germ sent me PLUS the very interesting "Final Flesh" & a People Like Us (Vicky Bennett [sp?]) movie - both pretty special & both sent to me by Germ.

etta came by & watched some of the above + the beginning of Bunuel's Phantom of

<u>Libert</u>y - wch both of us have seen before but neither of us remember.

<u>Monday, June 12th, 2006EV</u>

Had breakfast at etta's w/ the boat kids - including Dan, a new arrival who'd performed in the backyard at etta's before when she was out of town - a show Icky'd set up. Made a copy of the Cassette Mythos Audio Alchemy K7 for Dan since he's read the Cassette Mythos book.

Took some of the Boat Kids & Aurelia to see 3609.

Got more than enuf "Official" bklts today to fill the remaining LPs.

FINALLY went to the Boat Kids house & started shooting interviews: Evan, Zoe, Matt, Caleb, Amy.

Dan gave me a K7 in trade.

Organized the Wid<u>ém</u>outh stuff at 3609 (although I want to change it eventually).

Suzie & Jasmine & Julie came by 3809.

<u>Tuesday, June 13th, 2006EV</u>

Sent off the IMP ACTIVISMs to Doug.

Julie tipped me off that there was a bike being thrown out wch I then went & got.

"Boat Kid" Ben came by & gave me filmstrips & their soundtracks & a copy of the <u>Kon</u>

Tiki bk & replaced the mandolin string he broke yesterday.

Met the Boat Kids at the Rock Room & took them back to my 3609 house & showed them 2 short filmstrips of mine. "Boat Kid" Evan helped me carry 2 end tables & a couch that were being thrown out.

Laura Trussell called me & we talked for an hr or so.

Linda Burnham emailed me.

Wednesday, June 14th, 2006EV

Wrote "Remembering Peter Pan" & mailed a copy of it to Dee Dee.

Worked extensively on the "Book 'Em" documentary.

Finished watching the last 3 movies on the People Like Us (Vicki Bennett) DVD that Germ sent me. Decided to add 1 of the movies to my Favorites list on-line.

Watched the TV Sheriff and the Trailbuddies "WVF" DVD that Germ sent me. Intense scratch mixing. Added this to my favorites list too.

Thursday, June 15th, 2006EV

Worked ever-so-slightly on the "Book 'Em" doc & the (M)Usic rm at 3609.

Got 2 new movies from Eide's: Robert Anton

Wilson: maybe logic & The Valley
(Obscured by Clouds).
Finished reading Vonnegut's Hocus Pocus.
Talked w/ a nice cameraman friend of Hyla &
Mark's who was videoing an Interfaith
Conference at the Warhol.
etta came by for pizza & we started watching
The Valley.
Didn't drink alcohol.

Friday, June 16th, 2006EV

Listened to my Usic - $\sqrt{-1}$ LP again for the 1st
time in a long time & once again
(egotistically?) concluded that it's
probably the greatest 'sound art' record
ever made.
Finished a 43:49 version of "Book 'Em" doc (&
then changed ti 42:08).
Redid "Remembering Peter Pan" so that it's a
smaller file (w/ pix) so it can be emailed
in full form & sent it out.
Started reestablishing friendly contact w/ John
Berndt - partially as a side-effect of
Peter Pan's unfortunate early demise.
Showed my proof of footnotes to neighbor Greg,
who liked it, & he told me that he was in
Baltimore where he met Neil Feather &
Greg told me that Neil sent me a new CD
via Greg.
Showed etta the "Book 'Em" doc & she liked it &
laughed alot.
Got the THUS CD from Greg & listened to it!
Hoopla!
Finished watching The Valley.

Saturday, June 17th, 2006EV

Made multiple copies of "Book 'Em".
Ate at Lulu's.
Grocery shopped.
Talked w/ Jeanine on the phone.

Sunday, June 18th, 2006EV

Now that "Book 'Em"'s finished, I've assembled all the basic materials for IMP ACTIVISM 7 & that's been assembled into a Final Cut Pro project. Let the even more massive editing job begin!
Worked more on the 3609 (M)Usic rm, library, attic, & backyard.
Finally got around to ordering 3 new batteries for the camcorder.
Went to the 3 Rivers Arts Festival screening that Tony Balko organized that has "Haircut Paradox" in it. Only stayed for the 1st half, an hr & 15 minutes or so. It was a strong program.
Stopped off at Kalie's & ate some delicious sushi she made & talked w/ her & Marissa.

Monday, June 19th, 2006EV

Got more stuff for 3609 & moved a little more stuff there & decided to shelve cassettes in an extremely compacted way stretching from the projection/living

rm to the (M)Usic rm & built a shelf relevant to that.
Worked a little on the massive IMP ACTIVISM 7.
etta came by & we watched all (etta didn't fall asleep during it!) of a Bollywood love story fairy tale film entitled <u>Paheli</u> - 1 of the few I've seen to use special effects.

Tuesday, June 20th, 2006EV

Finished building the shelves for my K7s at 3609.
Got pd $50 fpr the TRAF screenings by Tony Balko & hung out at Filmmakers talked w/ Tony & Steve Boyle.
Got the cheap food & booze at the Rock Room.

Wednesday, June 21st, 2006EV

Sortof finished putting the K7s on shelves & got the (M)Usic rm ready for playing in.
Made substantial progress on IMP ACTIVISM 7.
Julie came by & we talked for awhile.
Michael Pestel came to town & he & Elizabeth Panzer & I played at 3609. GREAT FUN!!
Elizabeth gave me her 2 CDs.
Didn't drink alcohol.

Thursday, June 22nd, 2006EV

Finished making "Capitalism is an Ism", a side-
    project that grew out of IMP ACTIVISM
    7, & screened it for Amy Moon & etta.
Helped etta put the roof rack on her tour car &
    made 41 Hollow Sister CDs for the tour
    too.
Finished reading <u>the dying poem</u> by Rob Budde -
    wch I picked up in Toronto last fall
    because it's on the great Coach House
    Press.
Read all of Jeremy Needle's <u>Elizabeth Must Die</u> -
    my 3rd bk on SIX GALLERY PRESS.

Friday, June 23rd, 2006EV

Worked on IMP ACTIVISM 7.
Rc'vd substantial packet of publications from
    jUStin!katKO.

Saturday, June 24th, 2006EV

Rc'vd large packet of CDs from John Berndt.
Finished IMP ACTIVISM 7.
Hung out w/ Julie.
Finished reading Michael Crichton's <u>Prey</u>.

Sunday, June 25th, 2006EV

Found some mistakes in IMP ACTIVISM 7 &
    corrected them & succeeded in
    transferring it from computer to VHS.

Finally started working on the 3609 attic clothes rack(s).
Witnessed <u>Robert Anton Wilson maybe logic</u>.
Made a DVD of the 1st part of IMP ACTIVISM 7 (it 'had' to be broken into 2 parts for the DVD).

Monday, June 26th, 2006EV

Finished one half of the clothes rack in the 3609 attic & hung my shirts on it.
Started building a shelf at 3609 intended for vaudeos.
Put carpet down in the 2nd floor hallway in 3609 (Whoopee!. right?! - OK, so it was a big deal for me!)
Met Matt & his friend Alina (Ally) riding bikes & showed them the latest 3609 developments.
Made some CDs for John Berndt.
Dumped the June 21st session into the computer & made 4 CDs of it.
Finally checked out the "Wrestling Team" DVD.

Tuesday, June 27th, 2006EV

Transferred the 1st 15 sections of IMP ACTIVISM 7 to mini-DV (it'll have to broken up into 3 tapes).
Talked w/ Greg on the phone & he turned me on to YouTube wch I signed up for as "idioideo".
Ed-Um finally (& unexpectedly) returned the

equipment he borrowed.

Once again corrected <u>footnotes</u> & burned discs of the latest.

Met Suzie & Matt & some of the boat kids at the Rock Room.

Finally [there're alotof "finally"s in this POSITIVE - implying that I've achieved some sort of closure or overcoming of procrastination] started checking out a bit of the Disinformation Conference (or what have you) DVD.

Continued my systematic listening to the CDs JB sent me.

Wednesday, June 28th, 2006EV

Made the IMP ACTIVISM 7 sleeve packaging & printed it out.

Talked w/ Eric Fleischauer.

Talked w/ Doug Retzler about his Autoternatives show some more.

Started working on "Play Out Regress explained" for PLANTARCHY.

Started planning a possible IMP ACTIVISM retrospective of excerpts at the Warhol Museum after talking w/ Greg about it.

Didn't drink alcohol.

Thursday, June 29th, 2006EV

Tracey Mortimore called bright & early about

coming by today to look at the various jobs.

Spent a coupla hrs taking posters down from the walls of 3809 in prep for more moving.

Started working on a new set of meta-samples.

Eric F came by & gave me a Videonics Titlist & a 3/4" deck & returned the DVD player & remote to me & we hung out & talked.

Tracey came by & gave me an estimate about the various jobs that I'm looking to get done around the 2 (or 3) houses.

Went to the Boat Kids place & shot a little more & saw where they plan to launch from.

Witnessed the entirety of the Bollywood <u>My Wife's Murder</u>.

<u>Friday, June 30th, 2006EV</u>

Got a good paycheck from the Warhol today SO I sent off 4 packages & bought hardware supplies for 3609 & media supplies & food.

The possibility of having an IMP ACTIVISM screening at the Warhol is developing.

Shot good boat launching footage w/ Dan & Amy. Great fun!

Julie's back. I picked her up at the bus stn & we had 2 beers at the Rock Room.

Drank this night but didn't drink 7 days this mnth.

<u>Saturday, July 1st, 2006EV</u>

Made a 2 part DVD set of IMP ACTIVISM 7 broken into chapters.

Shot more footage of the Boat Kids including of the launching of Ben's barrel raft.

Had some new folks that're friends of Amy & Dan's come by & I screened "Cuntralia" & the short version of "Harps & Angles" for them & saw a movie by people Dan knows.

Made 2 more IMP ACTIVISM 7s on VHS - direct from the Final Cut Pro file.

Didn't drink alcohol.

Sunday, July 2nd, 2006EV

Made more IMP ACTIVISM 7s on VHS - direct from the Final Cut Pro file.

Made new 'business' cards & gave some away.

Vaudeo-interviewed Dan & Amy in their mobile home.

Went to the Beelen St performance where Amy & Dan played (I shot a little of this) & where the 2 dancers who'd watched my movies from the nite before gave a pretty good performance. One of Gina's bands performed there too & the fiddle player from that group, Mandy, was friendly to me. All sorts of folks that I didn't even know were in town were there: Devon, Johnny, Carlin, Paul (from Philly), etc. I gave Mary Mack a copy of IMP ACTIVISM 7 to give to Pete to check out for the proposed Warhol gig. Hung out w/ Ron at Beelen St too. It was one of the best social events I'd been to for a while.

Monday, July 3rd, 2006EV

Got a chisel for tearing apart the 3809 kitchen ceiling.
Made another IA7.
John Allen called me from his retreat in West Virginia & we had a long talk & he invited me to participate in some projects of his.
Didn't drink alcohol.

Tuesday, July 4th, 2006EV

Vaudeoed David Meieran's Pittsburgh War Profiteers Ride.
Started working on downloading the April 22 Nudist Party footage.
Didn't drink alcohol.

Wednesday, July 5th, 2006EV

Doug Retzler called me & talked w/ me more about his Autoternatives show. I sent him & Bill Daniel an email to try to connect the 2.
Fixed the toilet at 3609 & finished the attic closet & moved some clothes there.
Finished reading PLANTARCHY ONE.
Finished reading Maurice Sandoz's The House Without Windows (w/ illustrations by Salvador Dali).

Thursday, July 6th, 2006EV

Took more clothes to 3609.
Food shopped in prep for boat trip.
Got an email from Dee Dee Taylor thanking me
    for my "Remembering Peter Pan".
Got permission from Andy B to use part of his
    "Wrestling Team" movie in the very
    hypothetical IMP ACTIVISM 8.
Shot a tiny bit at the Boat Kids river camp.
Been emailing back & forth w/ Bill Daniel.
Had a long & very interesting phone conversation
    w/ Jona.
Emailed Jona the Language Experiment materials.

Friday, July 7th, 2006EV

Went downriver for 6 hrs on Rob's pontoon boat
    & then rode my bike back 14 miles. We
    went as far as past the 1st lock (my 1st
    experience going thru a lock as far as I
    can recall) & I shot a good amt of
    footage. Rob gave me his "The Strange
    Voyage of the Leona Joyce" book about
    his boat trip last yr.
Didn't drink alcohol.

Saturday, July 8th, 2006EV

Had a long talk w/ Alisa.
Went to what's left of the Boat Kids' river camp
    & shot a little more.
Continued my systematic listening to the
    Volunteers Collective tapes (the

unedited originals) - wch I'm enjoying alot.

Read all of "The Strange Voyage.." wch was very informative.

Listening to these old Volunteers Collective tapes from '89 to '93, I'm beginning to realize that I've been a much more 'accomplished ' 'musician' than I (perhaps) ever gave myself credit for previously. In particular, my drumming on VC VI (w/ Chris Astier) &, particularly, my drumming on the end of the 2nd side of the tape of VC X (w/ Jack Wright) are damned good. The latter duet is about as good as anything I've ever heard along those lines of 'free jazz'.

Sunday, July 9th, 2006EV

Woke up at 3:20AM from an interesting sex dream.

Started thinking about editing together a "Hitting Things Some More" tape because I'm realizing that I have many good recordings of me playing percussion that aren't on the "Hitting Things" double CD set.

Left around 4:30AM to go & shoot footage of the launching of Ben's barrel raft & the other 3 boats leaving.

Decided to use the dramatic beginning &/or ending of Volunteers Collective XIII (my duet w/ Jeanine Farrell) as part of the soundtrack to this Boat Kids movie & entered it into the computer for that

purpose.
Made stills from the beginning of the footage of
David Meieran's "War Profiteers" tour &
emailed them to him.
Went to the Heinz plant to photo & video the
giant ketchup bottle sign there in the
daytime to use in the Boat Kids movie.
Recorded the end duet of Volunteers Collective X
into the computer for the proposed
"Hitting Things Some More" collection.
Talked w/ Jeanine on the phone.
Finally stopped procrastinating on making the
concrete pad for the hypothetical new
electric hot water heater. I didn't do a
very good job but at least I got it over
w/.
Went back to the Heinz plant to video the giant
ketchup bottle sign there in the
nighttime.
Endured the Uke of Phillips DVD.

Monday, July 10th, 2006EV

Awoke 6AMish from a dream in wch I was
travelling in an urban landscape & there
was another guy who looked pretty fried
who apparently was suffering
aftereffects from a drug he'd taken that
were causing him to hallucinate
'ordinary' inanimate objects to be other
more animate ones of a sortof gritty
shadowy appearance - wch I cd see too.
I tried to assure him he'd be ok. The
police were after him, perhaps because
he was acting oddly on the streets, & he
shapeshifted into a baby that was in my

arms to get away from them. We went into a sortof strip club where the girls were laying in bunk beds stacked somewhat high that had very little vertical distance between them & he turned into something resembling a slice of pizza. He was demonstrating that he could incorporate w/ me & share all his abilities. We were on top of one of the bunk beds & one or more of the girls complained that I hadn't even shared my slice of pizza w/ them (or some such). Then we sortof flowed to the floor where I may've shapeshifted into a baby & our plan was to find a girl I was attracted to so I cd flow inside her & fuck her. We/I were/was crawling across the floor & there was a sortof old-fashioned (ie 19th century bike) that had different sized wheels on the front & back & I decided that I wanted to fuck the girl who rode that who I had somehow surmised was out in front of the club so we were headed there. My companion was going to demonstrate something like how he cd explore the molecular structure of some object 1st & then I woke up.

Listening to Volunteers Collective XIX, "Vexations", part 1, I'm finding that I'm very much enjoying it. The combination of Rob's steady flow of Satie on prepared piano + my samples (etc) works very well. I've decided to pull off a part of this where I'm using the percussion samples. I'm once again conscious that I've been enjoying the duets I've been listening to: w/ Chris Astier, Jack Wright, Jeanine Farrell, & now Rob Johnston. I think I'll pull out the 2 duets Neil & I played at his & Valerie's party when the Official Project was in transition from the quintet to the big band in the spring of 1991. Hopefully I can find some drumming on one of those 2 sessions worth using on the "Hitting Things Some More" comp - something that, in these early stages, is 'in need' of some surprising archival material outside the VC canon that I've been concentrating on listening to.

Picked a part from VCs I, VI, & XIII for "Hitting Things Some More".

Set up direct deposit for my unemployment benefit checks.

Valentina called me.

Breen called to offer to take me to meet the Boat Kids even though she didn't go w/ them for more than a partial day. Bless you, BREEN!

Ken Glanden & Neil Feather both emailed me.

Didn't drink alcohol.

Tuesday, July 11th, 2006EV

Breen kindly gave me a ride to join the Boat Kids. This (eventually) consisted of Joy, Ben, Matt, Dan & Amy, Evan, Dre, Caleb & Ian, & Gina (some had left before I got there but we connected later). Joy worked on "Cody" (his barrel boat w/ the song written on it) wch he managed to actually row around in. Arrived at Beaver River (Creek?) where we caught up w/ Rob & camped at "Toilet Beach" aka "Dead Muskrat Beach". Interviewed Dre.

Wednesday, July 12th, 2006EV

Stayed most of the day at Toilet Beach where Joy continued to amuse us all w/ Cody before he had to return to Pittsburgh. Interviewed Ian. Went "Night Floaty", ie: travelled downriver at night, so we cd escape Dead Muskrat Beach. Tied up to beached runaway pier by zinc plant.

Thursday, July 13th, 2006EV

Got off to a fairly early start from the zinc plant beach. I dared to go swimming from the boats while they were motoring on the river. Had my 2nd experience going thru a lock. Camped at a small creek & went into a nearby town to go to a bar.

Friday, July 14th, 2006EV

Went to East Liverpool, Ohio. Some of the Boat Kids were interviewed there by a reporter from the East Liverpool Review. Hung out w/ Dre who I got to know much better & whose company I enjoyed. Finished reading Robert Shea's borderline romance novel <u>All Things Are Lights</u>. Got invited to Cluster Island by Bill where we partied most of the night & entertained the island inhabitants w/ the Boat Kids music. A woman named Suzie was the life of the party there.

Saturday, July 15th, 2006EV

Started reading <u>Kon Tiki</u>. Left Cluster Island accompanied by island resident Ken & finally met up at land owned by Brin's parents w/ the Boat Kids who had left 2 days earlier than this bunch + others who had come upstream from Wierton, WV: David Eberhardt, Gerty, Auralee, Ariel, Pete, Eric, Paula, Savannah, Zoe, Wendy & Dave, Bruce, Jacqueline, & Danica. Brin was there but cdn't come on the trip. While we were en route, we met people who'd read the E Liverpool Review article & were enthusiastic about it. Interviewed Ken. Had a long intense wonderful conversation w/ Jacqueline who I 'fell in love w/'.

Sunday, July 16th, 2006EV

Vaudeoed Jacqueline's improvised dance "Exercise in Vulnerability" wch was great & wch will be a major part in the Boat Kids movie (provisionally entitled <u>Unexpectedly Irrelevant Title</u>).

Monday, July 17th, 2006EV

Abandoned Cody & left Brin's place. Camped at Buffalo Creek.

Tuesday, July 18th, 2006EV

Left Buffalo Creek. Recorded my playing Leadbelly's "Bourgeois Blues" in Evan's boat - 1st time I'd played it in about 33 yrs. Interviewed Danica & Savannah. Camped before Wheeling. Interviewed Lee, & Dave.

Wednesday, July 19th, 2006EV

Interviewed Eric, Wendy, & Gerty. Shot the last of my Boat Kids footage in Wheeling WV.
Returned to P-Burgh for only $18 on a Greyhound.
Came home to more phone messages & emails than I'd usually expect.

Thursday, July 20th, 2006EV

Emailed Carolyn Lambert about possibly joining her on the Ohio.
Got my film/slide-strip back from the most

recent nudist mask party & from the
Boat Kids.
Picked up 4 cheap videos - including <u>Lifespan</u> w/
the Terry Riley soundtrack.
Ordered some vaudeos from Tape World so I can
finally put IMP ACTIVISM 7 to a good
quality 160.
Talked some more w/ Doug Retzler about
Autoternatives & decided to hook him
up w/ Carolyn Lambert.
Suzie & Jasmine came by briefly.
Started putting the Boat Kids interviews into the
computer.
Put the "Bourgeois Blues" as sung on Evan's boat
into the computer, extracted the audio,
turned it into an MP3, & sent it to John
Berndt as a part of my email
correspondence w/ him today.
Wrote to the East Liverpool Review to ask about
getting copies of the issue relevant to
the Boat Kids. [but their spam filters
blocked the message so I wrote to the
Boat Kids suggesting they try]
Endured the poorly acted <u>Lifespan</u>.
Finished editing <u>Hitting Things Some More</u>.
Didn't drink alcohol.

<u>Friday, July 21st, 2006EV</u>

Got 5 more utility shelving units for 3609 &
finished building the one for vaudeos
that I started there about a mnth ago.
Grocery shopped at Donatelli's in Bloomfield wch
was surprisingly cheap.
Got a postcard from etta.
Made the K7 'master' of <u>Hitting Things Some</u>

<u>More</u>.
Didn't drink alcohol.

Saturday, July 22nd, 2006EV

Learned from reading <u>Kon Tiki</u> that "maitai" (my favorite alcoholic drink) is Polynesian for "to like" (or some such).
Finished reading <u>Kon Tiki</u>.
Started reading Rob's <u>Open Eyes Unlock Doors</u>.
Worked more on the shelves for 3609.
Went to the movie theater to see <u>A Scanner Darkly</u>.
Talked w/ John Allen.

Sunday, July 23rd, 2006EV

Built more megashelving at 3609.
Moved another 2 vanloads to 3609.
etta's back.

Monday, July 24th, 2006EV

Moved another vanload to 3609.

Tuesday, July 25th, 2006EV

Moved another 2 vanloads to 3609.
etta took me out to eat.
Communication between David Galloway (of BookSurge) & myself seems to be enabling progress on <u>footnotes</u>.

Hung out w/ 3611 neighbor Mark & Jess & Adam of the Brereton folks at the Rock Room.

Wednesday, July 26th, 2006EV

Endured talking w/ the 3809 landlady enuf to get a few details worked thru somewhat.
Diddled a wee bit at 3609.
Checked out Craig Baldwin's <u>Spectres of the Spectrum</u>.

Thursday, July 27th, 2006EV

Arranged for the utilities to be shut off & transferred from 3809 to 3609.
Moved 2 vanloads - including my bed & dresser to 3609.
Got emails from Jacqueline Jensen today!! Wonderful.
Ben Grubb called me tonight from Marietta, OH, tonite just to talk! Wonderful.
Finished watching the Disinformation disc 2.

Friday, July 28th, 2006EV

Moved 3 vanloads to 3609 & worked a bit on the bedroom there.

Saturday, July 29th, 2006EV

Had dinner at etta's.
Got an email from Okra - the 1st communication
    I've had from him in yrs!
Kelly Stiles called.
Didn't drink alcohol.

Sunday, July 30th, 2006EV

Moved 4 vanloads to 3609.
Hung out w/ Julie.
Got my tattooing equipment & gave it to Crust
    for his 29th birthday.
Didn't drink alcohol.

Monday, July 31st, 2006EV

Went back to work at the History Center for
    what may be the 1st time in mnths.
Went w/ Julie to get a utility shelf for 3609 &
    got drunk together at Kelly's Bar where
    a friend of hers named April bought us a
    drink w/o even telling us she did it.
I don't remember how many days I didn't drink
    when w/ the Boat Kids but I reckon it
    was at least 3 days wch makes for a
    total of approximately 12 days this
    mnth.

**[During the last wk or 2 I've been considering
    stopping writing this POSITIVE diary as
    of today - not because it's no longer
    positive to continue it, eg, but more
    because having stuck to it for a yr seems
    sufficient & because stopping it now will
    give me a feeling of closure. This diary**

encapsulates a clearly significant period of my life: the rise & demise of my relationship w/ Germaine (who I now have ceased communicating w/ for the longest time since I've know her: 3 wks), the (still-in-progress) publishing of <u>footnotes</u> (my most substantial bk project yet), the phasing out of my employment at the Warhol Museum, my brief but passionate crossing paths w/ Valentina, my 1st purchase of a house, & my moving out of 3809 (where I've lived longer than anywhere I've ever lived since I was a child). Regarding this latter, it's noteworthy that I'm typing this w/ the laptop on the floor of the 3809 bedroom - this computer being one of the last traces of my life here. Almost everything else has been moved to 3609. I've slept the past few nites on a blanket on the floor. My breakfast this morning was eaten off a plate on the floor - the folding table & chair used in the kitchen having been moved out too. I'm writing this in the morning before leaving for work. Tonite will probably be the last nite I sleep at 3809. Tomorrow the phone gets switched to the new house. This move, even though it's physically the shortest distance move I've probably ever made, is a major move psychologically. This diary has often been minimally utilitarian - perhaps making my life seem more eventless than it's actually been. This has partially been because I've usually left working for other people for money out of it - so whole days have been reduced to an entry like "Didn't drink alcohol", eg. Movies that I've witnessed that haven't been that great have been omitted - such as <u>One Hour Photo</u> wch I just checked out a few nites ago. Much of the diary has consisted of a simple noting of the beginning, progress, & ending of various projects - as usual showing my goal oriented thinking. Less has been written about the significance of these projects - wch is where the 'meatier' content wd potentially be. Has this project been a 'success'? Probably yes. It's been a success in the sense that it kept me focused on at least *TRYING* to perceive some part of every day in a positive 'light'. Hopefully this attitude will continue after the cessation of POSITIVE. I'm somewhat (ever the qualifiers!) confident that it will because a yr of dedication to such a process is a pretty powerful inculcator.]

Made in the USA
Middletown, DE
15 October 2024